CLEAN
ARCHITECTURE

A Comprehensive Beginner's Guide to Learn the Realms of Clean Architecture from A-Z

ELIJAH LEWIS

TABLE OF CONTENTS

Introduction

S uccess in software development requires architecture as much as a building project, for example. Software architecture proposes better organization, quality in performance, reliability, system portability, impacting non-functional requirements directly.

The Layered Architecture

Layered architecture came up with the idea of separating presentation from business logic from the software. This way of organizing software development is to split the application into layers to separate responsibilities and make the software easier to maintain and reuse.

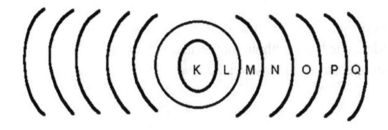

For the architecture of small software, usually, three layers are listed:

- **UI (User Interface)** - UI layer makes interaction and presentation of data to the user;

- **Business Logic Layer (BLL)** - Business Layer stores logic, dealing with software business rules, also called business logic layer or domain layer.

- **DAL (Data Access Layer)** - Data Access Layer: responsible for accessing and persisting application data;

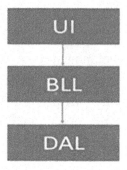

The operation of this architecture provides the following operation, and the interface layer should contain the pages to interact with the user obtaining information from the business layer, which in turn handles the application business rules and obtains information from the data access layer. The interface layer cannot know anything about the data access layer.

The purpose of this architecture is to create the possibility to change or update one layer without interfering with the other layer, based on a level of abstraction between the layers.

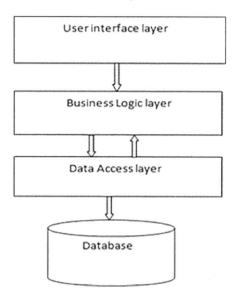

Looking at the diagram on the left, it is clear that the order of the three layers mentioned imposes a dependence of the upper layer to the lower one. Which can generate a possible problem in this form of traditional architecture? Designed in this order, software developers may have difficulty when making any changes to the System Database. They may make it difficult to test business logic code because it depends on the data access layer.

There are currently many architectures that rely on layered architecture, some increasing the number of layers, replacing or reversing the order of certain layers to bring more benefits to meeting non-functional requirements. Amid layered architecture, and the need for software changes came to The Clean Architecture.

The Clean Architecture

The clean architecture created by Uncle Bob (Robert C. Martin), represented by a diagram with concentric circular layers, is based on the isolation of these layers, so that replacement of components in the layer is easy and does not affect the entire system.

The Clean Architecture

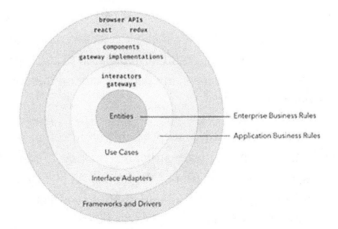

Swapping one component for another should not make the software work differently, or even stop working. Layer responsibilities are defined as follows:

Framework and Drivers

It is the outermost layer, protects the system from changes in detail, i.e., changes in this layer do not imply software functionality, so it is the detail layer and communicates with the next inner circle.

Interfaces Adapters (Adapters Interface)

Converts user-entered data into a structure that interacts with the system, where the presenters, controls, gateways, and repositories reside.

Application Business Rules (Application Business Rules)

It is responsible for processing information, where use cases are, where business rules are validated, and feedback on what is happening.

Corporate Business Rules (Enterprise Business Rules)

The layer of entities where business-level business rule codes are. These codes must be ready for reuse.

In the Clean Architecture proposal, all dependencies must point inwards; the outer circles are mechanisms and inner politics. In other words, the source code should not be aware of the layers external to your layer, should not have any dependency on these so the name of Dependency Rule.

The whole division and concept of this architecture provide a better organization of the software structure, making it easier for possible changes, due to the isolation of the layers. At any time, the interface components may be modified and in no way affect the meaning and operation of the software.

Chapter One

The Road To Software Architecture - Hexagonal, Onion and Clean Architecture

Are you interested in software architecture? I hope so because this is one of those aspects that should interest you regardless of your level of experience in the world of software development. If you are a junior programmer, you should be interested in it as soon as possible if you want to evolve as a professional.

You cannot consider yourself a senior or analyst without knowledge of the subject. A team leader, a Scrum Master, a QA, a CTO, or any business role will need to know, to a greater or lesser extent, and aspects of the systems architecture. This ensures they understand its scope, ensure its maintainability, the ability to reuse components, code quality, scalability, and cost of future migrations, assess technological dependencies, extensions, etc.

Ok, it is clear that architecture is important, but when you read "Software Architecture," what comes to mind? Maybe you think "I have to put the batteries with ..." and you get words like REST, SOAP, frameworks like Spring, Vaadin or JSF, data storage with Hibernate, MongoDB, Elasticsearch, or maybe other NodeJS, Websockets, Angular. It is even possible that you think of Docker, Amazon AWS... because in my opinion, I think you are going badly.

All this is nothing more than technologies, tools. Who tells you where they will be in 5 years, or even in 5 months. Your architecture must be prepared to adapt to the changes. "Modularity" and "business logic" will be the keywords.

The first thing we need is a way to structure the code of business applications with a high level of complexity to maximize modularity and separation of responsibilities. Then the technologies will come.

In recent years there is much talk about the concepts of Hexagonal Architecture, Onion Architecture, and Clean Architecture. They are confused and assumed as one thing, but they are not exactly the same. They have a chronological order of appearance and each one is based on the previous one and tries to improve it.

In this chapter, I will give you an introductory summary of these three concepts that start the path of yellow tiles towards clean software architecture.

Hexagonal Architecture

In 2005 Alistair Cockburn proposed the concept of "Hexagonal Architecture," also called "Ports & Adapters" architecture (Ports & Adapters).

The idea, roughly, is based on the construction of software systems based on a series of ports (public access interfaces) and adapters (implementations of those interfaces for a specific context) that communicate with the core of the application, That is where all the business logic is.

This seeks to implement business logic (the core) in isolation and independent of any external agent. The ports and adapters are the points of entry, exit, and conversion of data. There will be an adapter for each external agent: an adapter for the user interface

(UI), another for persistence, another for the execution of tests, another for communication with other services, etc.

In this way, more reusable, more modular, and more maintainable systems are achieved. And the way to achieve this decoupling is through the principle of dependency inversion.

Create your application to work without a user interface or database, only so that it can be executed by automatic regression testing. However, this concept alone seems to me too abstract.

The hexagonal architecture does not establish any structural code rule. Nor does it pose restrictions on interaction between components. Can a UI component communicate directly with a persistence component?

Or should you do it through the core? Perhaps we should assume all this as a conceptual framework or set of good practices rather than as architecture itself.

Onion Architecture

In 2008 Jeffrey Palermo introduced a new concept that he calls "Onion Architecture."

The author himself defines it as "an architectural pattern" that seeks to avoid one of the major drawbacks of using the traditional three-layer architectures: the coupling between the layers. According to Jeffrey, the traditional approach creates systems where the user interface cannot work without business logic, and business logic cannot work without data access. And as a consequence, the user interface is coupled to data access.

To avoid these links, it proposes an architecture based on circular layers like an onion. A fundamental rule will restrict this entire layer system: all code can depend on the most central layers, but cannot depend on the layers farthest from the core. That is, all the coupling is towards the center.

Each layer will have a specific responsibility:

- **Application core:**

  - **Domain Model:** In the center will be the domain model, which represents the objects and states of the organization.

  - **Domain Services:** Interfaces that define behaviors and operations on the domain model.

  - **Application Services:** Interfaces that define specific behaviors of the application.

- **External Elements:** In the outermost part is the user interface, the infrastructure, and the test system. The outer layer is reserved for things that can change more often. These things should be isolated from the core of the application. For example, the interfaces defined in the service layers would be implemented here. These implementations will have technological dependencies.

Onion architecture is based on these four principles:

- The application is built around an independent object model.

- The inner layers define the interfaces. The outer layers implement those interfaces.

8

- The direction of the coupling is always towards the center.

- The entire core code of the application can be compiled and executed in isolation to the infrastructure.

Both the hexagonal architecture and the onion architecture share the following premise: externalize aspects of infrastructure and the existence of an adaptation code that allows this infrastructure to be independent.

Clean Architecture

And finally, in 2012, Uncle Bob, in his already famous article, introduces the concept of "Clean Architecture."

"The first concern of an architect is to make sure that the house is usable, not to make sure that the house is made of brick." (Uncle Bob)

Uncle Bob realizes that, in short, all these concepts and architectures are based on the same idea: the separation of layers. And it focuses its attention on the fact that they all coincide in two things: in considering the business logic layer as the main axis of the system and in defining a series of interfaces to communicate with the rest of the system. You can call it Domain, Business Logic, Core, Application, or whatever you want. Still, in any case, this layer is the most important, the one that handles the threads, and everything must be designed and modularized around it. So Uncle Bob decides to include these proposals in a single concept that he calls "Clean Architecture" and summarizes the characteristics that a system built with this type of architecture must have:

- Independent of frameworks. The architecture should not depend on any framework or library whose characteristics condition our system to its requirements and restrictions. The frameworks should be taken as support tools.

- Testable. Business logic must be able to be tested without the need for any external activity (user interface, database, web server, etc.).

- UI independent. The graphical user interface should be easily replaceable without affecting the rest of the system (for example, changing a web UI for a desktop UI, and even for a console interface, it should not involve any changes to business logic).

- Independent of the database. Similar to what happens with the UI, the database must also be easily replaceable. The business rules must remain outside the persistence system, no matter if we use Oracle, SQL Server, MongoDB, or a simple file system.

- Independent of external factors. In short, business logic should not have direct knowledge of anything that comes from the outside world (the mode of communication with other systems -REST, SOAP, RMI, etc.), the server where it runs -Wildfly, Glassfish, Tomcat, etc.-).

Following its intention to unify criteria, Uncle Bob integrates all these architectures into a single idea represented by the following scheme:

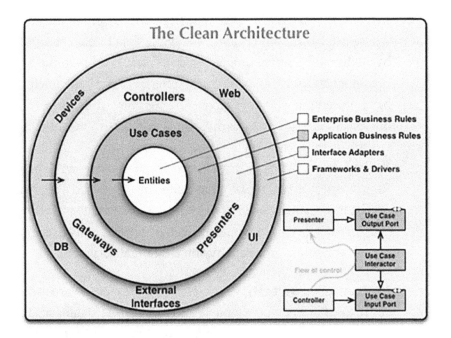

Each circle represents an area of the software:

- **Enterprise Business Rules:** Area that encapsulates business logic at the enterprise level. Here will be the objects, data structures, and/or functions that allow modeling all business logic. Entities of type Person, Group, Order, Line of Order, Invoice, etc. They will be part of this layer. Eye, do not confuse with the JPA Entities!

- **Application Business Rules:** Area that contains the application-specific business rules. Here the use cases that our application makes on business entities are implemented. While the previous layer dealt with the actors, it deals with the interactions (associating a Person as a member of a group, creating an Order with Line Items). Changes in this layer should not affect the entities instead of a modification in the entities if it can affect the use cases.

- **Interface Adapters:** Area that contains a set of adapters where use cases convert understandable data to data accepted by external elements, and vice versa. For example, to communicate with the graphical interface, we will need to have presenters who are responsible for converting objects of our business logic to specific objects of the framework that we are using for the UI (JSF, Spring, Swing, Vaadin ...). With respect to the persistence system, we will have Repositories that make that adaptation based on the persistence system used (ORMs, JPA, Hibernate, MyBatis ...). Another example would be SOAP service converters, or JSON structures, provided by some external service.

- **Frameworks and Drivers:** The most external area that consists of frameworks and tools such as the database, the web framework, testing systems, etc. Here are all the details. The web is a detail. The database is a detail. We keep these things out where they can't do much harm.

And finally, here I indicate some considerations, rules, and restrictions posed by this architecture:

- Dependencies should only point inward to inner layers or circles. An inner layer should not know anything about a higher-level layer.

- Flow control between layers is achieved by applying the principle of dependency inversion. Thanks to this principle (of which Uncle Bob is also the author) we can ensure that source code dependencies do not affect the flow of control

- The data that cross the boundaries between layers are simple data structures or DTO (Data Transfer Objects). For example, entities or rows of a database could not cross these boundaries since we would transmit dependencies, even if they are simple annotations (as is the case with JPA Entities within the Java EE world).

- They do not have to be strictly four levels, and they can be more as long as the previous rules are fulfilled.

As you can see, it also says nothing new, but if it puts a little order in this whole idea of decoupling from the principle of dependency investment.

At the moment, the concept of "Clean architecture" seems a compilation of best practices based on other previous concepts and ideas (and the author's own experience). The main improvement that seems to have contributed to the community is a more detailed and precise definition of the layers, rules, restrictions, considerations, and characteristics that a software architecture must have to be considered "clean."

But the word "clean" goes much further, enough to write a book and now we are going close the trilogy with this book on "Clean Architecture" where, apart from explaining in greater depth what is seen in this chapter, you will get answer questions of the type:

- What are the basic principles of software architecture?

- What is the role of a software architect?

- What makes architecture go wrong, and what can we do about it?

- And much more

In my view, the main advantage of this type of approach is that of postponing technological decisions, which is a consequence of

13

modularization. We can start implementing the core as soon as we know what the application is about. Imagine you start a project.

It is still unclear whether it will be a web application or an APP for smartphones. It is also not known if you want to persist the data in a relational or NoSQL model. What is known is that you will have to handle users, orders, invoices, a shopping cart, etc.,. well, what to expect! Let's start implementing the core, and let's save time until business clears up.

Another of the main advantages is to minimize the impact of the changes. This is also a consequence of modularization, of having everything well separated and responsibilities well distributed.

On the other hand, we must bear in mind that such an architecture makes sense in large applications. In a small application without prospects for enlargement, it can even be counterproductive. It makes no sense to complicate things over the account.

Chapter Two

Software Architecture
Design Patterns And Its Benefits

What is Architecture?

The SAR defines architecture as:

1. f. Art of designing and constructing buildings.

2. f. Design of a construction.

Applying it to the world of software development, we could redefine software architecture such as:

1. f. Art of designing and building computer applications.

2. f. Design of a computer application.

The definition we give to architecture comes from the world of construction, but it comes to mean the same in our world, only that we don't build buildings, we build software.

What is Software Architecture?

Software architecture defines the way you work in a system, such as building new modules, but you must also intuit the type of application you describe. As Uncle Bob comments, if we show an architectural drawing of a church or a floor, simply by looking at the shape of that drawing, we can intuit what type of building he is projecting. So, if we look at our architectural software drawing, we should be able to intuit what kind of application is going to be built. An application that controls a hospital is not the same as an application of an ATM, and each would have a different architectural drawing.

However, the architectural drawing in the construction does not make clear the materials with which it is made, likewise in the architectural drawing of our system, and we should not miss details of our implementation.

Thus, I consider the architectural drawing in a software project the very structure of modules and folders or packages in the case of Java or any addition that helps to express the intention of our system without expressing how it is made.

Uncle Bob also defines a series of "clean architectures" that have a series of objectives in common:

1. Independent of the frameworks. The existence of this way of building things in the system does not depend on a framework.

2. Testable. Your architecture makes your code can be tested.

3. Independent of the UI. A UI requirement does not alter your business rules, and when you develop new functionality, it is the UI that adapts to your business rules and never the other way around.

4. Independent of the database. You can change the persistence engine since your business rules are not dependent on the concrete implementation of the database, but it is the database that adapts to these rules.

5. Independent of any external component. The same rule described in the database applies but related to external components as well as integrations with other systems, libraries, etc.

If a software architecture meets these objectives, it could enter the group of clean architectures.

Use Cases

A use case is an action that an external user or agent performs in our system. They are always named with a verb + name. If we were developing an application in which products are sold, it ListProducts would be a valid name as well BuyProduct.

A common way to identify the intention of our system is to model it based on its use cases. They are the way to access the business rules of our application. Therefore we could say that they represent the public part of the domain of our application. Being the public part, they make input/output data to the domain.

The use cases help us to express in a more natural language the possible actions that our system can perform and thus list the functionalities of it. A list of use cases ordered by functionality will help us know what the application we are working with is about. For example, in Java, if we distribute the use cases separated by the functionality package, it will give us that vision of architectural drawing that we were talking about at the beginning of the chapter.

To do the action, they will talk with internal elements of our domain, such as services or rich model objects, so that through their collaboration, they resolve the action.

These use cases are thus the input element of our application and control the sequence of steps of the internal elements with which they collaborate. To solve a use case as BuyProduct, perhaps in our system, the input data must pass through a validating object, and in the case that the data is valid to keep that object in persistence, so those two steps would be correlated in the case of use.

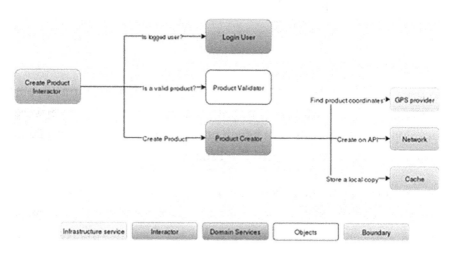

Business Rules

A business rule is a requirement of the manager to define how an application works, in Agile, we use the role of the Product Owner. They define the behavior of our system and how it reacts to actions by a user or an external agent if it had to interact with other systems. Business rules add value to the system we are building.

As we have described so far, our business rules are the core of our architecture. It all depends on these rules since we create software to offer a solution to a need.

Why is it so important to separate our business rules? The software evolves, the frameworks, database, libraries that we use are only tools with which we build a system. But as they evolve, the way they are used changes or they are even replaced by better ones, and it will be much easier to replace these new ones tools in our system if they are as isolated as possible.

There is only one rule to use a clean architecture, the dependency rule. This rule expresses that the dependency between components of our system must be from the implementation details to our domain and never let our domain know these details. This is the tool we have to isolate what adds value to our application from the implementation or technologies we use.

But your Product Owner is hardly going to explain exactly the rules of your business, express what you expect to find or how the application will react in a certain case. We are the developers responsible for translating your language and extracting business rules and Model the application based on what we call a domain data model; the domain is the business we are talking about.

This art of transforming a specification into something tangible in the development of the system is difficult, and you don't have to worry about it not being perfect at first. It is something that should be in continuous evolution as knowledge about the domain is gained, so we call this continuous refinement.

To make this continuous refinement, we have to change parts of our system so that they clearly reflect the intention. If we change parts of our system, we should be sure that we are making changes without damaging others, for that we need our architecture to be testable.

Testing

All this separation between business rules and other parts of our system make our components testable as we communicate the pieces that make up this puzzle with abstractions. The abstractions are our allies when composing these pieces because they provide us two clear advantages: give semantic meaning to a class employee and invest dependence to mocker a collaborator on the test.

This dependency inversion also allows us to change the detail of a class's implementation, which makes our architecture independent of the tools we mentioned previously since we have to distinguish between what to do (abstraction) and how to do it (implementation).

Independent of External Agents

Our application, as we have said, must be independent of external agents such as frameworks, databases, UI, external APIs, or other systems that we have no control. To comply with this rule, we must be clear that any external agent can be harmful since, at any time, it can be replaced by another that can fulfill the same mission in our system.

Any framework or library that makes us develop code using forms that are not standards in the language we are developing should be covered with an abstraction, so if in the future we want to change that library for another or even implement it ourselves we can do it alone making a change in how the implementation is created for that abstraction

This is also applicable to other external agents such as databases, which only fulfill a mission in our system, which is to persist objects. Our system is only interested in persisting the object X but not in the way it is implemented. That is why an abstraction also gives our code semantics because the abstraction, in this case, would be called XDataStorerand could be implemented in multiple ways depending on the technology we want to use.

Implementing an architecture helps us to understand better what our software is about to focus on the mastery of our application, which is the real value, and that, after all, is the reason that leads us to write software. Implementing a rich model based on our domain means that all team members have the same vocabulary and strength to give names to concepts, which makes understanding easier. It also makes it easier for our code to be more maintainable, testable, and consequently helps us to comply with SOLID principles.

Software Design Patterns

The purpose of this section is to present a theme that, in recent years, has gained the attention of the software community, which is charged every day to design better quality software solutions at the lowest cost. One way that undoubtedly contributes to achieving quality if software projects are design patterns.

In the course of the text, a definition of what it is will be presented, and what characterizes a design pattern, and it is clear to show that overuse can lead to the inverse situation that the design patterns propose.

Currently, a serious software development process is not conceived without the use of object-orientation, since it allows adding important qualities to the systems developed under its paradigms, such as extensibility and reusability, get those qualities.

To create the best solutions, you need to follow a detailed process for an analysis of requirements, functional or non-functional, and develop a design that satisfies them and enables them to be tested for possible flaws, plus if you wish to that the project has a flexible architecture to accommodate future problems and requirements without the need for redesign.

By analyzing the daily development of software, it is possible to identify that the search for a solution to a specific problem has identical characteristics, if not the same as that found in a previously developed project, but that due to the process deficiency, the solution and the problem were not documented.

And sometimes so little understood in its entirety, making it impossible to reuse ideas and solutions. Thus, identical problems that are repeated in other contexts are not recognized as such, consuming time and resources in search of solutions that, in theory, had already been found.

One thing advanced designers know they shouldn't do is to solve every problem from elementary principles or from scratch. Instead, they reuse solutions that have worked in the past and use them repeatedly in their projects. It's like solving a previously unheard of a mathematical problem, or at least unknown to someone.

First, we use all the knowledge and mathematical principles that are known, and that will be useful in the solution. After some attempts and use of the mathematical theories, we arrive at the solution and from there we have an "algorithm" (assembled structure that can be used to solve so many problems that exist and is identical to the solved one, and even if it is not, it is possible to reuse the ideas and conclusions of the solved problem.) That's why design patterns, design patterns,

Design patterns make it easy to reuse successful solutions and architectures to build object-oriented software flexibly and easily. Using design patterns can reduce the complexity of the software design process. In addition, well-designed object-oriented software enables designers to reuse and employ pre-existing components in future systems.

In software, design patterns are neither classes nor objects. Instead, designers use these patterns to build sets of classes and objects. To use them effectively, designers need to become familiar with the most popular and effective standards used by software engineering and to know their context and scope.

The idea of designing solutions from something already known and documented is not new. It has no origin in the software industry, although it already shows an interest in the subject. The idea came up in 1977 when Christopher Alexander published a catalog of more than 250 standards for civil architecture, discussing common architectural issues, describing in detail the problem, and the justifications for its solution.

Christopher Alexander found that by lowering focus, by looking for structures that solve similar problems, he can discern similarities between high-quality designs. He called these similarities "patterns."

Sometime later he formalizes his method of describing patterns, arguing that their use would not limit architects to prescribed solutions, but would guarantee the presence of fundamental elements, and the possibility of perfecting them through acquired experience. This method caught the attention of the software community, making the theme stand out in object-oriented conferences.

In 1995 Erich Gama, Richard Helm, Ralph Johnson, John Vlissides, known as the four friends [Gang of Four - GoF], published the book on the title: "Design patterns - elements of reusable object-oriented software, Addison Wesley Longman,"

Setting Design Defaults

Defining what a design pattern is clearly and objectively has been the goal of the software community since the 1980s. The first to present a definition of what would be a pattern was professor architect Christopher Alexandre, in his book "The Times Way of Building" (Oxford University Press, 1979). His definition is: "Each pattern is a three-part rule that expresses a relationship between a certain context, a problem, and a solution." Thus to understand the need, existence, of a pattern, it is necessary to study its parts: the problem, the solution, and the context to which it applies.

Thus, briefly, it can be understood as a design pattern, as the recurring solution to a problem in a context, even in different projects and areas. Note that the key terms of this definition are context, problem, and solution, which makes it imperative to understand each other unequivocally.

A context concerns the environment and the circumstances within which something exists. The problem is the undefined issue, something that needs to be investigated and solved. It is usually tied to the context in which it occurs. Finally, the solution refers to the answer to the problem that helps solve it.

However, if we have a solution to a problem in a certain context, it may not necessarily constitute a pattern, since it must be characterized by regularity, that is, it will be a pattern if it can be used repeatedly.

According to Christopher Alexander, "Each pattern describes a problem in our environment and the core of your solution so that you can use this solution more than a million times without ever doing it the same way."

The group of four friends classified the design patterns by two criteria. The first criterion is a purpose - it reflects what a pattern does. Patterns can have design, behavioral, and structural purposes.

Creation patterns describe techniques for instantiating objects (or groups of objects) and make it possible to organize larger classes and objects into the structure. Behavioral ones are characterized by the way classes or objects interact and distribute responsibilities, and structural ones deal with the composition of classes or objects. The second criterion is scope - specifies whether the pattern is applied to the class or object.

Characteristics of a Design Pattern

Although a pattern is a description of a problem, a generic solution, and its justification, this does not mean that any known solution to a problem can constitute a pattern, as there are mandatory characteristics that must be met by the standards.

They must have a name that describes the problem, the solutions, and the consequences. One name allowed me to define the vocabulary to be used by designers and developers at a higher level of abstraction.

Every pattern should clearly state to which problem (s) it should be applied, that is, which problems when inserted in a given context, the pattern will be able to solve it. Some may require preconditions.

The solution describes the elements that make up the project, their relationships, responsibilities, and collaborations. A pattern must be a concrete solution, and it must be expressed as a template (algorithm), which, however, can be applied in different ways.

Every standard should report what its consequences are so that the alternative project solution can be analyzed and the benefits of the project application understood.

A design code cannot be considered a specific code snippet; even if for its creator, it reflects a pattern that solves a particular problem because the patterns must be at a higher level of abstraction and not limited to programming resources. A design pattern names, abstracts, and identifies key aspects of a common design structure to make it useful for creating a reusable object-oriented project.

The Importance of Design Patterns

The most important thing about standards is that they are approved solutions. Each catalog includes only patterns that have been found useful by many developers in various projects. Cataloged standards are also well defined; The authors describe each pattern very carefully and in their own context, so it will be easy to apply the pattern in your own circumstances. They also form a common vocabulary among developers.

When Standards Won't Help You

Patterns are a map, not a strategic one. Catalogs will usually present some source code as an example strategy, so they should not be considered definitive. Standards will not help you determine which application you should be writing just how to implement the application best once the feature set and other requirements are determined. Patterns help with what and how, but not why or when.

The concept of using patterns indiscriminately is known as anti-patterns. According to Andrew Koenig, if a pattern represents "best practice," then an anti-pattern represents a "lesson learned."

There are two notions of antipatterns:

- Those who describe a bad solution to a problem that has resulted in a bad situation;

- Those that describe how to get rid of a bad situation and how to proceed from that situation to a good situation.

In short, an anti-pattern constitutes the misuse of design patterns, or their overuse, which can be seen by the use of patterns that are inappropriate for a given context, or improper use. Using patterns provides increased system flexibility. However, it can make it more complex or degrade performance. Some losses are tolerable, but underestimating the side effects of adopting patterns is a common mistake, especially those who take their use as a differential rather than the real need.

How Design Patterns Solve Design Problems

The primary target of using design patterns in software development is object-orientation. Since objects are the key elements in OO projects, the hardest part of designing is the decomposition of a system into objects. The task is difficult because many factors come into play: encapsulation, granularity, dependency, flexibility, performance, evolution, reuse, and so on. All of these influence decomposition, often in conflicting ways.

Much of the participating objects come from the method of analysis. However, object-oriented designs end up being composed of objects that have no real-world counterpart.

The abstractions that come up during a project are the keys to making it flexible. Design patterns help identify less obvious abstractions as well as the objects that can capture them. For example, objects that represent processes or algorithms do not occur in nature. However, they are a crucial part of flexible designs. These objects are rarely encountered during analysis or even during the early stages of a project; they are discovered later in the process of making a project more flexible and reusable.

How to Select a Design Pattern

Choosing from the existing standards, the one that best solves a project problem without making the mistake of making the wrong choice and making it unfeasible is one of the most difficult tasks. In short, choosing a design pattern to use can be based on the following criteria:

1. Consider how design patterns solve design problems.

2. Examine what the intent of the pattern is, i.e., what the design pattern actually does, what its principles are, and what particular design topic or problem it addresses (solves).

3. Study how patterns relate.

4. Study the similarities between the patterns.

5. Examine a cause of design overhaul.

6. Consider what should be variable in your project; that is, instead of considering what might force a change in a project, consider what you want to be able to change without redesigning it.

How to Use a Design Pattern

Once you have chosen the pattern (s) to be used in the project, you need to know how to use it. One approach recommended by the four friends gang to apply a pattern to a project is:

1. Read the pattern completely once to get your overview. Knowing the pattern especially its applicability and consequences is important for it to really solve your problem;

2. Study Structure, Participants, and Collaborations sections. Making sure you understand the classes and objects in the pattern and how they relate to each other;

3. Choose names for pattern participants that make sense in the context of the application;

4. Define the classes. Declare interfaces, establish their inheritance relationships, and define instance variables that represent data and object references. Identify the existing classes in the application that will be affected by the pattern and modify them;

5. Define application-specific names for operations in the pattern. Names generally depend on the application. Use the responsibilities and collaborations associated with each operation as a guide;

6. Implement operations to support the standard responsibilities and present collaborations. The Implementation section offers suggestions to guide you through implementation.

These are just guidelines that can be used until the experience and knowledge needed to develop a particular way of working with design patterns is gained. Design standards should not be applied indiscriminately. They often gain flexibility and variability by introducing additional levels of indirect addressing, and this can complicate a project and/or cost something in terms of performance. A design pattern should only be applied when the flexibility it offers is really needed.

Major Design Patterns

A quick read of Delphicon's Visual Component Library (VCL) code shows that it was built using design patterns extensively. Which is very good because it notes the level of excellence of the tool. This is because Delphi fully implements the good object-oriented practices - OOP, which assists in the implementation of reusable projects.

Breeding Patterns

Creation patterns are those that abstract or postpone the creation process of objects. They help make a system independent of how its objects are created, composed, and represented. A class creation pattern uses inheritance to vary the class that is instantiated, while an object creation pattern will delegate instantiation to another object.

Creation patterns become important as systems evolve to rely more on object composition than class inheritance. Object-based development enables objects to be composed without having to expose their interiors as they do in class inheritance. This enables dynamically defining behavior and the emphasis shifts from rigidly coding a set fixed behavior, to define a smaller set of behaviors that can be composed in any number to define more complex behaviors.

There are two recurring themes in these patterns. First, all encapsulate knowledge about which the system uses concrete classes. Second, they hide the way these classes are created and assembled. All the system generally knows about objects is that abstract classes define their classes. Consequently, design patterns give much flexibility in what is created, who creates, how, and when it is created. They allow you to configure a system with "product" objects that vary widely in structure and functionality. The setting can be static (that is, specified at compile time) or dynamic (at run time).

Abstract Factory

It is intended to provide an interface for creating related or dependent object families without specifying their concrete classes. Also known as Kit.

This pattern should be applied when one wishes to isolate the application from the implementation of the concrete class, which could be a specific component and framework in which the application would only know one interface and the concrete implementation would be known only at runtime or compilation.

Imagine that an application needed to be deployed to support different platforms and features — for example, one desktop view and one mobile view (Pocket PC phone). The way to build it would be to define a family of components for each platform and a factory that instantiates them according to the target platform on which the application will be running.

According to the four friends, the use of the Abstract Factory pattern should be restricted to the following situations:

- A system must be independent of how its products are created, composed or represented;

- A system must be configured as a product of multiple product families;

- A family of objects is designed to be used together, and you need to enforce this restriction;

- You want to provide a library of product classes and want to reveal only their interfaces, not their implementations.

The architectural structure of the pattern defined according to GoF is as shown in the Figure below.

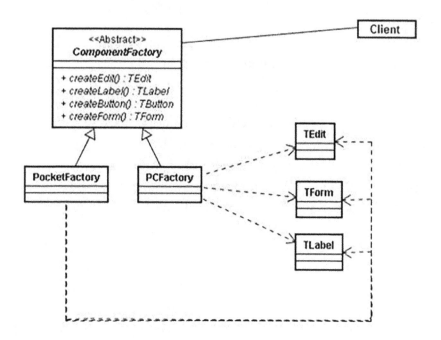

The structure of an example more in line with the developer reality is presented in Figure 2. The basic idea presented by the figure is to offer the user (developer) the possibility to run an application on different platforms.

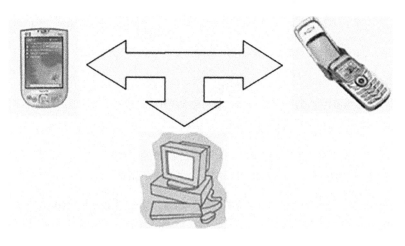

The participants are:

- **ComponentFactory** -declares an interface for operations that create objects of components used in the application;

- **PocketFactory** - concrete class that implements operations that create objects in the format of the client device;

- **PCFactory** -class -class that implements the operations responsible for creating objects in PC format.

The Abstract Factory pattern has the following benefits and disadvantages:

- It isolates the concrete classes.

- It makes it easy to exchange product families.

- It promotes harmony between products.

- It is difficult to support new types of products.

Factory Method

Define an interface for creating objects, but let subclasses decide which class to instantiate. Factory Method, also known as a virtual constructor, makes it possible to postpone object creation to subclasses.

This pattern is commonly used by software designers when there is a need to encapsulate the creation of a class by isolating itself from the knowledge of the client application's concrete class through an interface.

This need is commonly desired by those working on framework development, which use abstract classes to define and maintain relationships between objects. This way, customers implement the functionality expected by the framework by adding application-specific business logic, without the framework knowing how and what logic the application implements to complement it.

An example of using the pattern may be in building applications that have to support different persistence implementations with minimal rework.

Use of the Factory Method standard may be conditional when:

1. A class cannot anticipate the class/type of objects it must create;

2. A class specifies that its subclasses know the objects they create;

3. Classes that delegate responsibility to one of several helper subclasses, and you want to know which helper subclass the delegate is.

The participants are:

- **Product** - defines the object interface to be created by the factory method;

- **ConcreteProduct** - implementation of interfaceProduct;

- **Creator** - declares the factory method which returns an object of type Product;

- **ConcreteCreator** - overrides the factory method that returns a concrete instance of interfaceProduct.

The Factory Method standard eliminates the need to append application-specific classes to code. The code only deals with the Product interface, so it can work with any user-defined implementation of the class it implements, Product.

Singleton

Ensuring that an object will have only a single instance, that is, that a class will generate only one object and that it will be uniquely available for the entire scope of an application.

Some applications have to control the number of instances created of some classes, either for the sake of logic itself or for performance and resource-saving reasons.

Imagine when an application that exists simultaneously on a mobile device (Pocket PC, Mobile, Palm) and in a corporate environment needs a process of synchronization between the information processed on the mobile device and the corporate base. Both applications should communicate with an object that should be unique to process this timing to avoid the possibility of creating data in the database.

Use of the Singleton standard is subject to:

- When it is necessary to maintain in a system, whether distributed or not, only one object instance and that the access point for it is well known (e.g., object responsible for a print pool on a network, window manager);

- When the single instance has to be extendable through subclasses, allowing customers to use an extended instance without changing its code (polymorphic views).

- Delphi developers already use the default behavior Singleton in their applications, when they declare global variables in the startup project area, and then reuse the instance of objects. TApplication, TCiipInterface are examples of objects that would have no meaning; there is more than one instance of the application, and therefore, they assume the behavior of the Singleton pattern.

The structure of the pattern is shown in the Figure below.

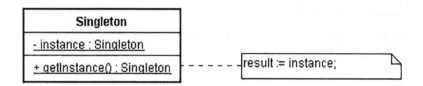

The participants are:

1. Singleton - defines a static method that allows clients to get a single object. He will also be responsible for the object creation process.

The benefits that the standard has been:

- Controlled access to single instance;
- Reduced namespace (say no to the proliferation of global variables);
- Allows refinement of operations and representations;
- Allows a variable number of instances - The standard enables the strategy of creating more than one instance of the class in a controlled manner;
- More flexible than class operations;

Structural Patterns

Structural patterns are concerned with how classes and objects are composed to form larger structures. Classes use inheritance to compose interfaces or implementations and object instead of composing interfaces or implementations, and they describe ways to compose objects for new functionality. The flexibility obtained by object composition comes from the ability to change composition at run time, which is not possible with a static composition (class inheritance).

Adapter

Convert the interface of one class to another expected by customers. This makes it possible for classes with incompatible interfaces to work together - or otherwise impossible. Also known as a Wrapper (adapter).

Sometimes a class of a toolkit designed to be reused does not match the domain-specific interface required by an application.

Use of the standard is subject to:

1. Use an existing class, but its interface does not match the required interface;

2. Create reusable classes that cooperate with unrelated or unanticipated classes, i.e., classes with an initially incompatible interface.

The participants are:

1. Target - defines the client domain specific interface;

2. Client - collaborates with Target compatible objects;

3. Adoptee - Existing interface needs adaptation;

4. Adapter –adapts interfaceAdoptee interfaceTarget.

For class adaptations:

- A class adapter will not work when we want to adopt a class and all its subclasses;

- Allows Adapters to replace some Adoptee behavior, as Adapter is a subclass.

For object adaptations:

- Allows a single Adapter to adapt to an Adoptee and its subclasses;

- It makes it harder to redefine the behavior of an Adoptee. Achieved through a subclass of Adaptee, which is a referenced adapter.

Behavior Patterns

Behavior patterns focus on algorithms and assignments of responsibilities between objects. They describe not only object or class patterns, but also patterns of communication between objects.

Class behavioral patterns use inheritance to distribute behavior among classes, and object behavioral patterns use object composition as opposed to inheritance. Some describe how object groups cooperate in performing a task that could not be performed by an object alone.

Template Method

Define the skeleton of an algorithm in operation by deferring some steps to subclasses. Template Method allows subclasses to redefine certain steps of an algorithm without changing its structure.

Now imagine that you have to build an application that has a certain function of which only the execution algorithm is known, and the coding work to perform the operation can be delayed. See the next Figure.

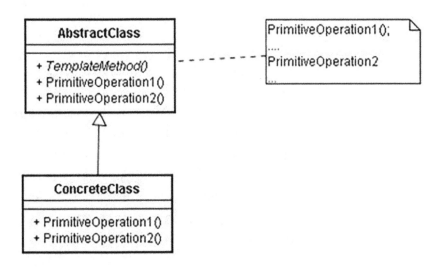

On the applicability of this standard we have:

- To implement the invariant parts of an algorithm and subclass the implementation of the variant part;

- To factor in similar behavior between subclasses in a superclass thus avoiding code duplication;

To control class extensions with hook methods

Its participants are:

- **AbstractClass** - defines the primitive and abstract operations that represent the steps of an algorithm and implements a method that invokes these primitive operations;

- **ConcreteClass** - implements the specific operations defined in the superclass with the specific code.

Template methods are a fundamental technique for code reuse. They lead to an inversion of control IoC framework or principle of inverse dependency, commonly known as the "Hollywood principle," meaning, "don't call us, we'll call you." This refers to how a parent class calls the operations of a subclass, not the other way around.

The use of design patterns enables the flexible construction of applications and/or code structures and the documentation of reusable solutions. Through design patterns, it is possible to identify the commonalities between two different solutions for the same problem. Knowing these commonalities allows us to develop even better and more efficient solutions that can be reused, thus enabling the advancement of human knowledge.

Patterns make it possible, through clear and concise language, for experienced designers to transfer their knowledge to the youngest at a high level of abstraction and thus facilitate code development and reuse.

Chapter Three

Clean Architecture: Architecture Oriented Development

Software, generally speaking, is an almost constant state of change. Changes occur because of the need to correct existing software bugs or add new features and functionality. Likewise, computer systems (i.e., those that have software as one of their elements) also change frequently. This evolving need for the software system makes it 'unreliable' and prone to defects, late delivery, and cost overruns. Concomitant with these facts, the growth in size and complexity of software systems requires professionals to reason, design, code, and communicate through software components. As a result, any system design or solution then moves to the architectural level.

Almost five decades ago, the software was a negligible part of existing systems, and its development and maintenance costs were negligible. To realize this, just look at the history of the software industry (see Links section). We find the use of software in a wide variety of applications such as manufacturing systems, scientific software, embedded software, robotics, and web applications, among many. At the same time, there was the emergence of various modeling and design techniques as well as programming languages. Note that the existing scenario decades ago has completely changed.

In the past, systems designs allocated a small portion of the software. Hardware components, on the other hand, were analyzed and tested almost exhaustively, which allowed the rapid production

41

of large numbers of subsystems and implied rare design errors. However, the ease of modifying software compared to hardware has served as a motivator for its use. In addition, the increased use of software in a wide variety of applications has made it grow in size and complexity. This has made it prohibitive to analyze and test it thoroughly and impact maintenance costs.

A reflection of this is that the abstraction techniques used until the late 1980s (such as modular decomposition, high-level programming languages, and abstract data types) are no longer sufficient to address this need.

Unlike the use of algorithms and data structures techniques and the programming languages that implement such structures, the growth of software systems demands notations for connecting components (modules) and describing interaction mechanisms, as well as techniques for managing configurations and controlling versions.

The following table shows the context of software architecture. In structured programming, sequence structures, decisions, and repetitions are used as 'patterns' of control in programs. Information hiding is a feature of the object-oriented paradigm that allows the programmer, for example, to hide data making it safe from any accidental change. Moreover, in object-oriented programming, data and functions can be 'encapsulated' into an entity called object, which results in more simplicity and ease of program maintenance. On the other hand, architectural styles capture the 'pattern' of organizing software components in a program, characterizing how components communicate with each other.

Approach	Focus	Standards
Structured Programming	Small systems	Control Structures
Abstraction and modularization	Midsize Systems	Information encapsulation and hiding
Components and Connectors	Large systems	Architectural styles

Software architecture context.

Note that the categorization, presented in Table 1, was intended to capture an overview of approaches applied to software systems. Nothing prevents, for example, the use of structured programming in large systems or the emphasis of an architectural style on a small system. However, this practice is not common.

Note that as the size and complexity of software systems increase, the design problem goes beyond data structures and computation algorithms. That is, designing the system architecture (or overall structure) emerges as a new problem. Architectural issues encompass organization and overall control structure, communication protocols, synchronization, component functionality allocation, and selection of design alternatives. For example, in web systems, a solution that has been employed makes use of multiple layers separating client components, application servers, web servers, and other applications (which may have access to this system).

This layered structuring aims to facilitate the allocation of functionality to components. Using layers supports flexibility and portability, resulting in ease of maintenance. Another notable feature of layered architecture is the use of standard interfaces to facilitate reuse and maintenance. Well-defined interfaces encapsulate already tested components (with defined functionality), a practice that allows reuse and also aids maintenance, as any necessary changes would be confined to that component.

Importance of Software Architecture

All of these factors comprise design at the architectural level and are directly related to system organization and therefore affect quality attributes (also called non-functional requirements) such as performance, portability, reliability, availability, and more. If we make a comparison between software architecture (characterized, for example, by layered style) and 'classical' architecture (relating to building construction), we can see that architectural design is crucial to the success of the system.

The following Table highlights aspects of design representation that capture the characteristic elements of the architecture while restrictions are associated with quality attributes and therefore serve as determinants in decisions of the architectural design. For example, while using multiple layers makes it easy to maintain a software system, it also contributes to degrading system performance. One tactic has been to reduce the level of coupling between components so as not to compromise system performance. Thus, if we adopt a reduction in the coupling level of the components, they will have less need for communication with each other, which results in better performance.

Architectural Categories	Project Representations	Restrictions
Classical architecture	Models, drawings, plans, elevations, and perspectives	Circulation, acoustics, lighting and ventilation pattern
Software Architecture	Templates for different roles, multiple views	Performance, reliability, scalability, and maintainability

Comparison of architectural aspects.

Today, software engineering processes require architectural software design. Why?

- It is important to be able to recognize existing common structures so that software architects (or software engineers performing the role of software architect - as per Table 3) can understand the relationships that exist in the systems in use and use that knowledge in developing new systems.

- Understanding architectures allows engineers to make decisions about design alternatives.

- An architectural specification is essential for analyzing and describing the properties of a complex system, allowing the engineer to have a complete overview of the system.

- Knowledge of notations for describing architectures enables engineers to communicate new designs and architectural decisions made to other team members.

It is noteworthy that, to understand the architecture, the software engineer must know the existing architectural styles, as presented below. The properties of each architecture, therefore, are dependent on the architectural style adopted. For example, using a standard notation such as UML helps in representing components and sharing project information.

These aspects serve as indicators of an early software engineering maturity. Other aspects include the use and reuse of existing solutions in the development of new systems. To this end, prototyping has been used in projects of an innovative nature (well before the implementation or acceptance of a product takes place).

In addition, increasing complexity and the number of system requirements makes it increasingly difficult to meet budget and schedule constraints. Today, companies have sought to incorporate software reuse strategy, emphasizing architecture-centered reuse for better system development results. Note that software architecture serves as a framework through which one can understand the components of a system and their interrelationships. In other words, it defines the system structure consistently for deployments as it is directly related to quality attributes such as reliability and performance.

The organization of components in a software system impacts the quality presented by it. For example, adopting a layered architecture serves to modularize the system as well as facilitate modifications. However, too many layers (4 or 5) can degrade system performance if there is a high degree of coupling between components.

Several benefits derive from incorporating software architecture as a 'guiding element' of the software development process. It should be noted that the architecture can:

- Provide reuse support - your defined and tested components can be reused in new applications.

- Underpin cost estimation and project management - The existence of a well-defined architecture allows the project manager to properly allocate tasks from, for example, component implementation and to better estimate the time and team size required to complete a project.

- The basis for consistency and dependency analysis - The software architect can verify that the adopted software architecture supports the desired quality attributes consistently and evaluate the level of dependence of the quality attributes on the architecture. To do so, he makes the architectural analysis that verifies the support offered by the architecture to a set of quality attributes (such as performance, portability, and reliability).

- Be used to determine system quality attributes - The software architect does the architectural analysis to determine the quality attributes. It is an iterative process.

- Act as a framework for meeting system requirements - Architecture helps define functional requirements, which comprise the software system's feature set, and non-functional requirements (or quality attributes) that determine user-visible characteristics such as performance, and reliability.

One question you might be asking yourself is: Why has only recently been the focus on software architecture?

The answer is simple: economy and reuse.

Previously there was no strong emphasis on the software engineering discipline, a fact that occurred with the maturing of this new area throughout the 1990s. Everything motivated the emergence of a new professional: the software architect.

Software Architect Skills

Note that the software architect plays a key role in the company's strategy. He needs to have deep knowledge of the domain, existing technologies, and software development processes. A summary of a software architect's desired skill set and the tasks assigned to it are presented in the next Table.

Note that prototyping is a common task where the architect develops a prototype to 'test' a possible solution. Simulation can be used when it needs to evaluate the support offered to a certain quality attribute, such as performance. On the other hand, experimentation can occur when the architect needs to test a newly implemented component.

Desired Skills	Tasks Assigned
Domain knowledge and relevant technologies	Modeling
Knowledge of technical issues for systems development	Commitment and Feasibility Analysis
Knowledge of requirements gathering techniques, systems modeling, and development methods	Prototyping, simulation, and experimentation

Knowledge of company business strategies	Technology Trend Analysis
Knowledge of processes, strategies, and products of competing companies.	'Evangelizer' of new architects

Skills and tasks of a software architect.

Understanding Architectural Style

The architectural style serves to characterize the software architecture of a system enabling:

- Component Identification - The architect identifies which key elements have well-defined functionality, such as a user information (registration) component and a user authentication component in a web application.

- Identification of interaction mechanisms - communication between objects through message exchange is one way in which software components interact with each other.

- Property Identification - The architect can analyze the properties offered by each style based on component organization and interaction mechanisms, as discussed below.

The architectural style considers the system completely, allowing the software engineer or architect to determine how the system is organized, characterizing the components and their interactions. In other words, it determines a structure for all system components. The architectural style comprises the vocabulary of components and connectors, as well as the topology employed. But you may be wondering: Why is knowing architectural style important?

Large systems require higher levels of abstraction (just where styles are) that support project understanding and communication between project participants. It is crucial in understanding the organization of a software system.

But, what is gained by knowing the architectural style? He offers:

- Support for quality attributes (or non-functional requirements);

- Differentiation between architectures;

- Less effort to understand a project;

- Reuse of architecture and knowledge in new projects.

Knowing the architectural style allows the engineer to anticipate, through (architectural) analysis, the impact that style (i.e., the system organization class) will have on quality attributes. Additionally, it facilitates project communication, as well as reuse of (solution) architecture.

The characterization and existence of architectural styles are signs of the maturity of software engineering since it allows the engineer to organize and express the knowledge of a project in a systematic and useful way. Note that one way of coding knowledge is to have a vocabulary of an existing set of concepts (terminology, properties, and constraints), structures (components and connectors), and usage patterns. Connectors are employed in the interaction between components such as pipe and filter style pipe and object style messages.

Exemplifying the Style Pipes and Filters

The architectural style of pipes and filters considers the existence of a network through which data flows from end to end. Data flows through tubes and data changes when processed in the filters.

who | sort

The above command line executes the who command (once) and forwards its output to the sort program, as illustrated in the next Figure. The result of running the who program is a list of all users who are currently logged on (to a specific server), while the sort program sorts this user list in alphabetical (login) order.

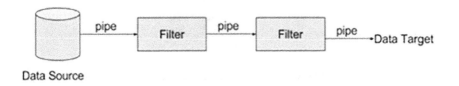

Data Source

Example of the architectural style of pipes and filters.

A compiler has two basic functions: analysis and synthesis. The analysis function is implemented by three components: lexical, syntactic, and semantic parsers. The synthesis function comprises the optimization and code generation components. Note that this architecture supports portability and reuse.

However, this architecture has evolved with the introduction of an intermediate code generator component to make the compiler architecture 'more portable' to multiple platforms to reduce costs in developing different products, or, i.e., compilers for different platforms.

A new evolution of compiler architecture to meet the need for (compiler) integration with other tools such as editor and debugger has resulted in the architecture.

Importantly, the evolution of the compiler architecture was mainly a result of the need to support the portability requirement. In this sense, it can be highlighted as advantages:

- Problem or system can be decomposed hierarchically;

- The system function is seen as filter composition;

- Ease of reuse, maintenance, and extension, which employs the black-box approach, where each component has well-defined functionality and interface, facilitating changes to them;

- Performance can be increased through parallel filter processing as component activation and use occur with data flow, allowing components with independent functionality to run concurrently.

Despite the advantages noted above, the tube and filter style emphasizes batch mode, making it difficult to use in interactive applications and situations requiring filter order. Another technical issue to note is the possibility of deadlock using finite buffers (for temporary data storage). This architectural style has been employed due to the advantages previously highlighted.

Examples of other Architectural Styles Include:
- **Layers** - The software system architecture is organized into a set of layers, offering greater flexibility and portability support. Identifying the level of abstraction is not always evident, and performance is lost as the number of layers

grows. An example of this style comprises the multilayer web systems that separate clients, application servers, web servers, and other web clients.

- **Objects** - This architecture combines data with functions into a single entity (object), facilitating problem decomposition, maintenance, and reuse. It is common to use object-oriented architecture in information systems such as online library consultation and lending systems that have user registration components and user authentication components. Note that similar components exist in other information systems, such as content sites (newspapers and magazines) that require registration and authentication by any user before making the content available.

- **Implicit Invocation** - Unlike the object-based style in which one component invokes another directly through message passing, implicit invocation requires components interested in receiving or disclosing events to register for receiving or sending. An example of a system employing messages is news and forum lists that have new user registration components coupled with the authentication component. Note that this type of system only allows the user to access content if it is properly authenticated and registered.

- **Events** - This is a style in which components can be objects or processes, and the interface defines the allowed input and output events. Connectors are implemented through the event-procedure binding. Thus, events are logged along with events, and the components interact with each other by sending events. Thus, when an event is received, the procedure (s) associated with that event is invoked. An interesting example of this style is online games, as discussed in the following section.

- **Blackboard** - This style makes use of a central data repository surrounded by a set of information components (or cells). These components contain information that is required for troubleshooting. Troubleshooting data is kept in the shared database (the repository), which is called the blackboard. The most common example of this style is an expert system.

- **Style Combination** - Other systems, in practice, combine architectural styles resulting in heterogeneity.

Exemplifying the Combined Style of Objects and Events

Online and computer games have now become commonplace with the popularity of the Internet. The games are usually categorized into:

- Turn-based: These are games in which each action is based on the player's turn as a tic-tac-toe game.

- Event-based: These are games where events can occur anytime, and they dictate the pace of the game. Examples include flight simulators and car racing.

For example, when games are made available on the Internet, they are commonly referred to as online games or Internet games, enabling the user to play against the machine (computer). An example of this type of computer game is Connect4, which aims for each player to connect four tiles of the same color, vertically, horizontally, or diagonally.

Each player must place a piece on the top of the selected column, as shown in the next Figure, and it falls until it fills the bottom column of the selected column. Note that the board contains seven columns and six rows, a game status indicator, and a manual selector (used to select the column into which a piece will be placed).

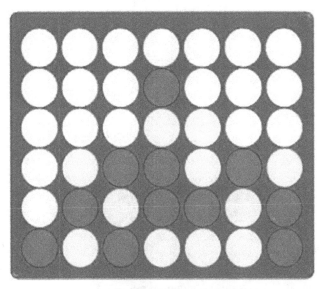

Connect4 game.

The software architecture of this application is presented in the Figure below. The computational player component (which has artificial intelligence capabilities to simulate a human player) contains a Connect4State class that handles most requests to check if a player has won the game, and also has a mechanism to update game status after a computational player's move.

The inference (machine) component contains a class for handling player moves as well as determining the best move for the computational player.

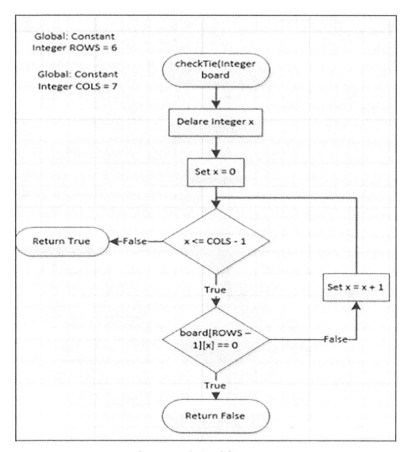

Connect4 Architecture.

The user interface component contains a class that loads the image and audio files, handles requests made via the mouse, and invokes a method that checks for victory, defeat or a draw, and updates the graphical interface. A possible final state of this game is shown in the next Figure, wherein the third row, there is a set of four pieces in blue color, indicating that the computer first completed the connection of four pieces in the same color (the human user's color is red).

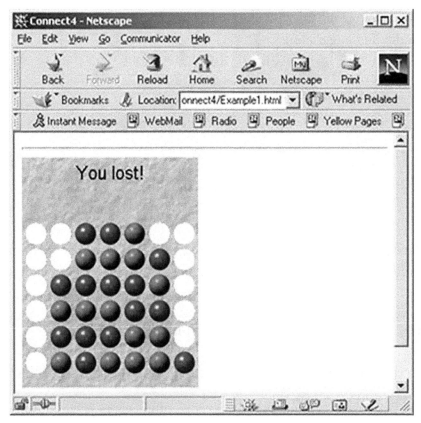

The possible final state of the game Connect4.

The combination of event and object-oriented architectural style allows the decomposition of a system in terms of objects (inference components, graphical interface component, and computational player component) that are more independent and enable computation and coordination (event) activities, are performed separately. There is also the ease of reuse and maintenance as new objects can be easily added. This feature, and well-defined interfaces, further facilitate integration.

The invocation mechanism is non-deterministic (i.e., occurs at random) as it considers the reception of events. Additionally, components have their data preserved from any accidental modification as this information is encapsulated in objects, also facilitating integration.

Importance of Reuse

It is important to understand from all that has been presented and discussed that an architectural model supports reuse in many ways. For example, you can have reusable architectures that provide the organization and coordination model, allowing them to be used across multiple systems. In addition, tested components can be reused on more than one system. Of all this, the most important is the reuse of knowledge that has a direct impact on defining the software architecture that is a candidate to solve a problem (or system).

The wide variety of platforms and utilities, coupled with market pressure to reduce software product delivery times, and increase productivity, make reuse one of the keys to success for companies.

Reuse of artifacts (or components) is possible when the architectural design is embedded and guides the software development process. This, as discussed, allows foreseeing the quality attributes that the system supports and also managing the project execution schedule. Therefore, positively impacting the reuse and economy of the system.

The table presented below summarizes the main characteristics of software architecture and important points in the training and retraining of software engineers and architects.

Software Architecture Features	Practical use of software architecture
It is a reusable artifact.	How a software architect can organize the design and code of a system
Has interconnection mechanisms	How an architect evaluates and deploys software architectures in systems
Provides project vocabulary and separates functionality	How a software architect acts in the software development process
Link design to quality attributes	How an architect evaluates code quality based on product metrics
Supports component-based and product line development (when requirements are considered for a family of systems)	Using architecture as a parameter to reduce maintenance costs and amortize development costs

Features and practical use of software architecture.

Although software architecture is a relevant theme in the current context for software system development that focuses on reuse and therefore considers both economics and productivity, its incorporation into software development processes has been observed only in enterprises of large and a few medium-sized.

However, this scenario is beginning to change, given the growing need for systems integration, which is premised on software architecture. Thus, the economic factor has been and will be the determinant of the survival of software companies. New systems development strategies should be for reuse and reuse (of software components), and the main pillar of these strategies is software architecture. There is, therefore, a pressing need for human capital formation with such qualifications.

Chapter Four

Principle In
Clean Software Architecture

The principle of sole responsibility is the first of the five that make up SOLID. If you hadn't heard about it until now, SOLID rules are the ABC of any expert developer. They are a set of principles that, applied correctly, will help you write quality software in any object-oriented programming language. Thanks to them, you will create code that will be easier to read, test, and maintain.

The principles on which SOLID is based are the following:

1. Principle of Sole Responsibility

2. Open / Closed Principle

3. Liskov Substitution Principle

4. Principle of Segregation of Interfaces

5. Dependency Inversion Principle

These principles are the basis of much literature that you will find around software development. Many architectures rely on them to provide flexibility, testing needs to rely on them to validate parts of code independently, and refactoring processes will be much easier if these rules are met. So it is very convenient that you assimilate these concepts well.

They were first published by Robert C. Martin, also known as Uncle Bob, in his book Agile Software Development: Principles, Patterns, and Practices. A person that I recommend you follow and take a look at his blog from time to time.

Principle of Sole Responsibility

The principle of Sole Responsibility tells us that an object must perform a single thing. It is very common if we do not pay attention to this, that we end up having classes that have several logical responsibilities at the same time.

How to Detect Violation of the Principle of Sole Responsibility

The answer to this question is quite subjective. Without obsessing with it, we can detect situations in which one class could be divided into several:

- **Two layers of architecture are involved in the same class:** it can be difficult to see without previous experience. In every architecture, however simple, there should be a presentation layer, one of business logic, and another of persistence. If we mix the responsibilities of two layers in the same class, it will be a good indication.

- **The number of public methods:** If a class does many things, it is likely that it has many public methods, and that they have little to do with each other. Detect how you can group them to separate them into different classes. Some of the following points can help you.

- **The methods that use each of the fields of that class:** if we have two fields, and one of them is used in a few methods and another in a few others, this may be indicating that each field with its corresponding methods could form an independent class. Normally this will be more diffuse, and there will be methods in common because surely those two new classes will have to interact with each other.

- **For the number of imports:** If we need to import too many classes to do our job, we may be doing extra work. It also helps to look at what packages these imports belong to. If we see that they are grouped easily, it may be telling us that we are doing very different things.

- **It is difficult for us to test the class:** if we are not able to write unit tests on it, or we do not achieve the degree of granularity we would like, it is time to consider dividing the class into two.

- **Every time you write a new feature, that class is affected:** if a class is modified often, it is because it is involved in too many things.

- **For the number of lines:** sometimes it's as simple as that. If a class is too large, try to divide it into more manageable classes.

In general, there are no golden rules to be 100% sure. The practice will let you see when it is recommended that a certain code be moved to another class, but these clues will help you detect some cases where you have doubts.

Example

A typical example is that of an object that needs to be rendered in some way, for example, by printing on the screen. We could have a class like this:

```
public class Vehicle {
    public int getWheelCount ( ) {
        return 4 ;
    }
    public int getMaxSpeed ( ) {
        return 200 ;
    }
    @Override public String toString ( ) {
        return "wheelCount =" + getWheelCount ( ) + ", maxSpeed ="
    + getMaxSpeed ( ) ;
    }
    public void print ( ) {
        System. out . println ( toString ( ) ) ;
    }
}
```

Although, at first glance, it may seem a most reasonable class, we can immediately detect that we are mixing two very different concepts: business logic and presentation logic. This code can give us problems in many different situations:

- In the case that we want to present the result differently, we need to change a class that specifies the form of the data. Right now, we are printing on screen, but imagine that you need to be rendered in HTML. Both the structure (surely you

64

want the function to return the HTML), and the implementation would change completely.

- If we want to show the same data in two different ways, we don't have the option if we only have one method print().

- To test this class, we cannot do it without the side effects of printing by the console.

There are cases like this that look very clear, but many times the details will be more subtle, and you probably won't detect them at first. Do not be afraid to refactor what it takes to fit what you need.

A very simple solution would be to create a class that is responsible for printing:

```
public class VehiclePrinter {
    public void print ( Vehicle vehicle ) {
        System. out . println ( vehicle. toString ( ) ) ;
    }
}
```

If you need different variations to present the same class differently (for example, plain text and HTML), you can always create an interface and create specific implementations. But that is a different topic.

Another example that we can often find is that of objects to which we add the method save(). Again, the logic layer and the persistence layer should remain separate. Surely we will talk a lot about this in future books.

The Principle of Unique Responsibility is an indispensable tool to protect our code against changes since it implies that there should only be one reason to modify a class.

In practice, many times, we will find that these limits will have more to do with what we really need than with complicated dissection techniques. Your code will give you clues as the software evolves.

Do you think you can apply it from now on in your day to day tasks?

In the following section of this chapter, I will talk about the Open/Closed Principle, the second of the SOLID principles.

Open / Closed Principle

After having looked at the first principle, the principle of sole responsibility, it is time to talk about the Open / Closed Principle, the second on the SOLID list:

- Principle of Sole Responsibility

- *Open / Closed Principle*

- Liskov Substitution Principle

- Principle of Segregation of Interfaces

- Dependency Inversion Principle

Open / Closed Principle

Bertrand Mayer first named the Open / Closed principle, a French programmer, who included it in his book Object-Oriented Software Construction back in 1988.

This principle tells us that a software entity should be open to extension but closed to modification. What does this mean? That we have to be able to extend the behavior of our classes without modifying their code. This helps us to continue adding functionality with the assurance that it will not affect the existing code. New functionalities will involve adding new classes and methods, but in general, it should not involve modifying what has already been written.

The way to get there is closely related to the previous point. If classes only have one responsibility, we can add new features that will not affect them. This does not mean that complying with the first principle will automatically comply with the second, or vice versa. Then you will see a clear case in the example.

The Open / Closed principle is usually resolved using polymorphism. Instead of forcing the main class to know how to operate, it delegates this to the objects it uses, so it does not need to know how to carry it out explicitly. These objects will have a common interface that they will implement specifically according to their requirements.

How to Detect Violation of the Open / Closed Principle

One of the easiest ways to detect it is to realize what classes we modify most often. If every time there is a new requirement or a modification of existing ones, the same classes are affected, we can begin to understand that we are violating this principle.

Example

Following our example of vehicles, we may need to draw them on the screen. Imagine we have a class with a method that draws a vehicle on the screen. Of course, each vehicle has its own way of being painted. Our vehicle has the following form:

```
public class Vehicle {
    public VehicleType getType ( ) {
```

```
    ...
  }

    ...

}
```

It is basically a class that specifies its type through an enumeration. We can have, for example, one enum with a couple of types:

```
public enum VehicleType {
  CAR,
  MOTORBIKE
}
```

And this is the method of the class that is responsible for painting them:

```
public void draw ( Vehicle vehicle ) {
  switch ( vehicle. getType ( ) ) {
    case CAR:
      drawCar ( vehicle ) ;
      break ;
    MOTORBIKE case :
      drawMotorbike ( vehicle ) ;
      break ;
  }
}
```

While we do not need to draw more types of vehicles or see that this switch is repeated in several parts of our code, in my opinion, you should not feel the need to modify it. Even the fact that you change the way you draw a car or motorcycle would be encapsulated in your own methods and would not affect the rest of the code.

But there may come the point where we need to draw a new type of vehicle, and then another. This implies creating a new enumeration, a new case, and a new method to implement the drawing. In this case, it would be a good idea to apply the Open / Closed principle.

If we solve it by inheritance and polymorphism, the obvious step is to replace that listed with real classes, and that each class knows how to paint:

```
public abstract class Vehicle {

   ...

   public abstract void draw ( ) ;

}
public class Car extends Vehicle {
   @Override public void draw ( ) {
      // Draw the car
   }
}
public class Motorbike extends Vehicle {
   @Override public void draw ( ) {
      // Draw the motorbike
   }
}
Now our previous method is reduced to:
public void draw ( Vehicle vehicle ) {
   vehicle. draw ( ) ;
}
```

Adding new vehicles is now as simple as creating the corresponding class that extends from Vehicle:

```
public class Truck extends Vehicle {
```

```
@Override public void draw ( ) {
    // Draw the truck
}
}
```

As you can see, this example directly clashes with the one we saw in the Principle of Unique Responsibility. This class is saving the object information and how to paint it. Does that imply that it is incorrect? Not necessarily. We will have to see if the method of drawing our objects negatively affects the maintainability and testability of the code. In that case, we would have to look for alternatives.

Although I am not going to present it here, an alternative to fulfill both would be to apply this polymorphism to classes that only have a method of painting and that receive the object to be painted by the constructor. We would, therefore, have one CarDrawerwho is responsible for painting cars, or one MotorbikeDrawerwho draws motorcycles, all of them implementing draw(), which would be defined in a parent class or interface.

When should we Comply with this Principle?

It must be said that adding this complexity does not always compensate, and like the rest of the principles, it will only be applicable if it is really necessary. If you have a part of your code that is prone to change, consider doing it so that a new change impacts as little as possible on the existing code. Normally this is not easy to know a priori, so you can worry about it when you have to modify it and make the necessary changes to fulfill this principle at that time.

Trying to make a 100% Open / Closed code is virtually impossible, and can make it illegible and even harder to maintain. I will not get tired of repeating that SOLID rules are very powerful ideas, but we must apply them where appropriate and without obsessing to comply with them at every point of development. It is almost always easier just to use them when the real need arises.

The Open/Closed principle is an indispensable tool to protect us against changes in modules or parts of code in which these modifications are frequent. Having code closed to modification and open to extension gives us maximum flexibility with minimum impact.

Did you know this principle? In what situations have you found it useful?

The following section will deal with the Liskov Substitution Principle, the third of the 5 SOLID principles.

You already read the Open/Closed principle, and now we are going to talk about the **Liskov replacement principle**:

- Principle of Sole Responsibility

- Open / Closed Principle

- *Liskov Substitution Principle*

- Principle of Segregation of Interfaces

- Dependency Inversion Principle

Liskov Substitution Principle

The Liskov substitution principle tells us that if somewhere in our code, we are using a class, and this class is extended, we must be able to use any of the daughter classes and that the program remains valid. This forces us to make sure that when we extend a class, we are not altering the behavior of the father.

This principle comes to refute the preconceived idea that classes are a direct way of modeling reality. This is not always the case, and the most typical example is that of a rectangle and a square. Soon we will see why.

The first to talk about him was Barbara Liskov (hence the name), a renowned American software engineer.

How to Detect Violation of the Liskov Substitution Principle

Surely you have encountered this situation many times: you create a class that extends from another, but suddenly one of the methods is left over, and you don't know what to do with it. The fastest options are either to leave it empty or to throw an exception when it is used, making sure that no one incorrectly calls a method that cannot be used. If an overwritten method does nothing or throws an exception, you are likely violating the Liskov substitution principle. If your code was using a method that for some concretions now throws an exception, how can you be sure that everything is still working?

Another tool that will let you know easily is the tests. If the tests of the parent class do not work for the daughter, you will also be violating this principle. With this second case, we will see the example.

Example

In real life, we are clear that a square is a rectangle with two equal sides. If we try to model a square as a concretion of a rectangle, we will have problems with this principle:

```java
public class Rectangle {

    private int width;
    private int height;
    public int getWidth ( ) {
        return width;
    }
    public void setWidth ( int width ) {
        this . width = width;
    }
    public int getHeight ( ) {
        return height;
    }
    public void setHeight ( int height ) {
        this . height = height;
    }
    public int calculateArea ( ) {
        return width * height;
    }
}
```

And a test that checks the area:

```java
@Test
public void testArea ( ) {
    Rectangle r = new Rectangle ( ) ;
    r. setWidth ( 5 ) ;
    r. setHeight ( 4 ) ;
    assertEquals ( 20 , r. calculateArea ( ) ) ;
}
```

The definition of the square would be as follows:

```
public class Square extends Rectangle {
    @Override public void setWidth ( int width ) {
        super . setWidth ( width ) ;
        super . setHeight ( width ) ;
    }
    @Override public void setHeight ( int height ) {
        super. setHeight ( height ) ;
        super. setWidth ( height ) ;
    }
}
```

Try now in the test to change the rectangle to a square. What will happen? This test is not met; the result would be 16 instead of 20. We are, therefore, violating the Liskov substitution principle.

How Do We Solve It?

Several possibilities depend on the case in which we find ourselves. The most common will be to expand this hierarchy of classes. We can extract to another parent class the common characteristics and make the old class father and his daughter inherited from her. In the end, it is most likely that the class has so little code that you end up having a simple interface. This is not a problem at all:

```
<
pre class = »»>
public interface IRectangle {
    int getWidth ( ) ;
    int getHeight ( ) ;
    int calculateArea ( ) ;
```

```
}
public class Rectangle implements IRectangle {

  ...

}
public class Square implements IRectangle {

  ...

}
```

But for this particular case, we find a much simpler solution. The reason why it is not true that a square is a rectangle is that we are giving the option to modify the width and height after the creation of the object. We can solve this situation simply by using immutability.

Immutability is a very interesting topic that I will discuss later in another book of this series. It consists of that once an object has been created, the state of the object cannot be modified again. Immutability has multiple advantages, including better use of memory (all its state is final) or security in multiple threads. But following the example, how does immutability help us here? Thus:

```
public class Rectangle {
  public final int width;
  public final int height;
  public Rectangle ( int width, int height ) {
    this . width = width;
    this . height = height;
  }
}
public class Square extends Rectangle {
  public Square ( int side ) {
    super ( side, side ) ;
```

```
    }
  }
```

From the moment of instantiation of the object, everything we do with it will be valid, whether we use a rectangle or a square. The problem behind this example is that the assignment of one part of the state magically modified another field.

However, with this new approach, by not allowing modifications, the operation of both classes is completely predictable.

Liskov's principle helps us to use inheritance correctly and to be much more careful when extending classes. In practice, it will save us many mistakes derived from our eagerness to model what we see in real life in classes following the same logic. There is not always exact modeling, so this principle will help us discover the best way to do it.

The fourth section of this chapter will deal with the **principle of interface segregation**. What do you think so far? Do you think it makes sense to apply these principles in your day to day development?

Principle of Segregation of Interfaces

We are already finishing the review of the SOLID principles. After seeing the Liskov Substitution Principle, today we enter fully into the Principle of interface segregation.

- Principle of Sole Responsibility

- Open / Closed Principle

- Liskov Substitution Principle

- *Principle of Segregation of Interfaces*

- Dependency Inversion Principle

Principle of Interface Segregation

The interface segregation principle comes to say that no class should depend on methods it does not use. Therefore, when we create interfaces that define behaviors, it is important to be sure that all classes that implement those interfaces will need and be able to add behaviors to all methods. Otherwise, it is better to have several smaller interfaces.

The interfaces help us to decouple modules from each other. This is because if we have an interface that explains the behavior that the module expects to communicate with other modules, we can always create a class that implements it so that it meets the conditions. The module that describes the interface does not have to know anything about our code and, nevertheless, we can work with it without problems.

The Problem

The problem arises when those interfaces try to define more things than they should, what are called fat interfaces. It will probably happen that the daughter classes will end up not using many of these methods, and they will have to be implemented. It is very common to throw an exception, or simply do nothing.

But, as we saw in some examples in the Liskov substitution principle, this is dangerous. If we throw an exception, it is more than likely that the module that defines that interface will use the method at some point, and this will cause our program to fail. The rest of the "default" implementations that we can give can generate side effects that we do not expect, and to which we can only respond by knowing the source code of the module in question, which we are not interested in.

How to Detect Violation of the Principle of Segregation of Interfaces

As I commented in the previous paragraphs, if when implementing an interface, you see that one or more of the methods are meaningless and you need to leave them empty or throw exceptions, you are likely violating this principle. If the interface is part of your code, divide it into several interfaces that define more specific behaviors.

Remember that nothing happens because a class now needs to implement several interfaces. The important point is that you use all the methods defined by those interfaces.

Example

Imagine that you have a music CD store and that you have modeled your products in this way:

```
public interface Product
{
  String getName ( ) ;
  int getStock ( ) ;
  int getNumberOfDisks ( ) ;
  Date getReleaseDate ( ) ;
}
public class CD implements Product {
  ...
}
```

The product has some properties that our CD class will somehow overwrite. But now you have decided to expand the market, and start selling DVDs too. The problem is that for DVDs, you also need to store the age rating because you have to make sure that you don't sell movies that are not suitable according to the age of the client. The most direct thing would be to add the new property to the interface:

```
public interface Product
{

    ...

    int getRecommendedAge ( ) ;
}
```

What happens now with the CDs? They are forced to implement getRecommendedAge(), but they will not know what to do with it, so they will throw an exception:

```
public class CD implements Product {

    ...

    @Override
    public int getRecommendedAge ( )
    {
        throw new UnsupportedOperationException ( ) ;
    }
}
```

With all the associated problems we have seen before. In addition, a very ugly dependence is formed, in which every time we add something to Product, we are forced to modify CD with things that it does not need. We could do something like this:

```
public interface DVD extends Product {
    int getRecommendedAge ( ) ;
}
```

And make our classes extend from here. This would solve the problem in the short term, but some things can continue without working too well. For example, if another product needs categorization by age, we will need to repeat part of this interface. In addition, this would not allow us to carry out operations common to products that have this characteristic. The alternative is to segregate the interfaces, and for each class to use what it needs. We would, therefore, have a new interface:

```
public interface AgeAware {
  int getRecommendedAge ( ) ;
}
```

And now our DVD class will implement the two interfaces:

```
public class CD implements Product {
  ...
}
public class DVD implements Product, AgeAware {
  ...
}
```

The advantage of this solution is that we can now have code AgeAware, and all classes that implement this interface could participate in common code. Imagine that you don't sell only products, but also activities that would need a different interface. These activities could also implement the interface AgeAware, and we could have code like the following, regardless of the type of product or service we sell:

```
public void checkUserCanBuy ( User user, AgeAware ageAware ) {
  return user. getAge ( ) > = ageAware. getRecommendedAge ( ) ;
}
```

What to do with Old Code?

If you already have code that uses fat interfaces, the solution may be to use the "Adapter" design pattern. The Adapter pattern allows us to convert some interfaces into others, so you can use adapters that convert the old interface into new ones. I will talk about the design patterns in depth later.

The interface segregation principle helps us not to force any class to implement methods that it does not use. This will avoid problems that can lead to unexpected errors and unwanted dependencies. It also helps us reuse code more intelligently.

In the following section, we finally end with the SOLID rules, speaking of one of the most interesting principles: the **Dependency Inversion Principle**.

Dependency Inversion Principle

If you were interested in the interface segregation principle, the last one of the SOLID principles is the **Dependency Inversion Principle**; it is probably the one that changes the way you program most once you start applying it.

- Principle of Sole Responsibility

- Open / Closed Principle

- Liskov Substitution Principle

- Principle of Segregation of Interfaces

- *Dependency Inversion Principle*

Dependency Inversion Principle

This principle is a basic technique and will be the most present in your day to day if you want to make your code testable and maintainable. Thanks to the dependency inversion principle, we can make the code that is the core of our application not dependent on the implementation details, such as the framework you use, the database, how you connect to your server. All these aspects will be specified through interfaces, and the core will not have to know what the actual implementation is to work.

The definition that is usually given is:

- High-level classes should not depend on low-level classes. Both should depend on abstractions.

- Abstractions should not depend on the details. The details should depend on the abstractions.

But I understand that it is only with this that you are not very clear about what we are talking about, so I am going to explain the problem a bit, how to detect it and an example.

The Problem

In programming seen from the traditional model, when a module depends on another module, a new instance is created and used without further complications. This way of doing things, which at first glance seems the simplest and most natural, will bring us many problems later, including:

- **The most generic part of our code (what we would call the domain or business logic) will depend everywhere on implementation details.** This is not good, because we will not be able to reuse it, since it will be coupled to the shifting framework that we use, to the way we have to persist the data, etc. If we change any of that, we will also have to redo the most important part of our program.

- **The dependencies are not clear:** if the instances are created within the module that uses them, it is much more difficult to detect what our module depends on and, therefore, it is more difficult to predict the effects of a change in one of those modules. It will also cost us more to be clear if we are violating some other principles, such as sole responsibility.

- **It is very difficult to do tests:** If your class depends on others and you have no way of replacing the behavior of those other classes, you cannot test it in isolation. If something in the tests fails, you would have no way of knowing at first glance which class is to blame.

How to Detect Violation of the Principle of Dependency Inversion

This is very easy: any instantiation of complex classes or modules is a violation of this principle. In addition, if you write tests, you will notice very quickly, as soon as you can not test that class easily because they depend on the code of another class.

You will be wondering then how you will do to give your module everything it needs to work. You will have to use some of the alternatives that exist to supply those dependencies. Although there are several, the most commonly used are through the constructor and through setters (functions that all they do is assign a value).

And then still responsible for providing the dependencies? The most common is to use a dependency injector: a module that is in charge of instantiating the objects that are needed and passing them to the

83

new instances of other objects. You can make a very simple injection by hand, or use one of the many libraries that exist if we need something more complex.

Example

Imagine that we have a shopping cart that what it does is store the information and call the payment method to execute the operation. Our code would be something like this:

```
public class ShoppingCart {

    public void buy ( Shopping shopping ) {

        SqlDatabase db = new SqlDatabase ( ) ;

        db. save ( shopping ) ;


        CreditCard creditCard = new CreditCard ( ) ;

        credit card pay ( shopping ) ;

    }

}
public class SqlDatabase {

    public void save ( Shopping shopping ) {

        // Saves data in SQL database

    }

}
public class CreditCard {

    public void pay ( Shopping shopping ) {

        // Performs payment using a credit card

    }

}
```

Here we are breaking all the rules we imposed at the beginning. A higher level class, such as the shopping cart, is depending on other high-level ones, such as what is the mechanism for storing information or for making the payment method. It is responsible for creating instances of those objects and then using them.

Think now what happens if you want to add payment methods, or send the information to a server instead of saving it to a local database. There is no way to do all this without disassembling all the logic. How do we solve it?

The first step, stop relying on concretions. We are going to create interfaces that define the behavior that a class must give to function as a persistence mechanism or as a payment method:

```
public interface Persistence {
    void save ( Shopping shopping ) ;
}
public class SqlDatabase implements Persistence {

    @Override
    public void save ( Shopping shopping ) {
        // Saves data in SQL database
    }
}
public interface PaymentMethod {
    void pay ( Shopping shopping ) ;
}
public class CreditCard implements PaymentMethod {

    @Override
    public void pay ( Shopping shopping ) {
        // Performs payment using a credit card
    }
}
```

Do you see the difference? Now we no longer depend on the particular implementation we decide. But we still have to keep urging it on ShoppingCart.

Our second step is to invest the dependencies. We are going to make these objects go through constructor:

```
public class ShoppingCart {


    private final Persistence persistence;
    private final PaymentMethod paymentMethod;
    public ShoppingCart ( Persistence persistence, PaymentMethod paymentMethod ) {
        this . persistence = persistence;
        this . paymentMethod = paymentMethod;
    }
    public void buy ( Shopping shopping ) {
        persistence save ( shopping ) ;
        paymentMethod. pay ( shopping ) ;
    }
}
```

And if now we want to pay by Paypal and save it on the server? We define the specific concretions for this case, and we pass them by the builder to the shopping cart:

```
public class Server implements Persistence {
    @Override
    public void save ( Shopping shopping ) {
        // Saves data in a server
    }
}
```

```java
public class Paypal implements PaymentMethod {
    @Override
    public void pay ( Shopping shopping ) {
        // Performs payment using Paypal account
    }
}
```

We have already achieved our goal. In addition, if we want to test now ShoppingCart, we can create Test Doubles for dependencies, so that we can test the class in isolation.

As you can see, this mechanism forces us to organize our code in a very different way than we are used to and contrary to what logic initially dictates. Still, in the long run, it compensates for the flexibility it gives to the architecture of our application.

And with this, I'm finishing this chapter on SOLID principles.

Chapter Five

Clean Software Architecture and Non-Functional Requirements

The organization of the software functionality of a system is made explicit through the software architecture. There are a lot of architectural styles that bring peculiar characteristics to each style, and these, in turn, can be combined to create new styles. The heterogeneity of architectural styles is healthy. In fact, this is due to the need for the architecture to support a set of sometimes conflicting requirements, including non-functional requirements, a topic addressed in this chapter.

Software architecture design is an essential step in the development of large and complex software systems. Within this context, software architecture is fundamental for the development of software product lines where there is a set of features designed and implemented from the same base (software) architecture. However, prior to the software architecture design stage, there is a need to survey the system requirements.

In general, the set of requirements of a system is defined during the early stages of the development process. Such a set of requirements is seen as a specification of what should be implemented. Requirements are descriptions of how the system should behave, and contain application domain information and restrictions on system operation.

During the requirements elicitation phase, a software designer or architect uses his or her experience to gather the requirements, seeking to identify characteristics of the system to be developed. In addition, domain information, along with existing architectural style information, can be used as data sources to assist in identifying requirements.

Another feature that can be used by the designer is to build scenarios. Usage scenarios support specific requirements and address both elicitation and requirements analysis. Once the set of requirements has been obtained, the software designer/architect will be able to start the software architecture project, as illustrated in the Figure below.

This process of requirements gathering and analysis, in conjunction with the use of scenarios, is used to support the definition of software architecture, as discussed throughout the chapter. It is important to note that the architectural design step may need to make use of usage scenarios or even a re-analysis to refine the architecture to be employed in the system to be developed.

The architecture-based development process considers software architecture as a process driving factor. This entails placing nonfunctional requirements associated with architecture as key aspects of the development process. Note that the development of an architecture-centric software system begins with a software architect who has a set of system requirements. At this point, we seek to identify which style or combination of these best supports these requirements and, therefore, derive a software architecture that meets the characteristics of the system to be developed. It is noteworthy that the complexity of a software system is determined both by its functional requirements - what it does - and by non-functional requirements - as it does.

Functional Requirement

A software system requirement that specifies a function that the system or component must be able to perform. These are software requirements that define system behavior, that is, the process of transformation that software or hardware components perform on inputs to generate outputs. These requirements capture functionality from the user's point of view.

Non-Functional Requirement

In software system engineering, a nonfunctional software requirement is one that describes not what the system will do, but how it will do it. Thus, for example, you have performance requirements, external system interface requirements, design constraints, and quality attributes. The assessment of non - functional requirements is made, in part, by testing, while another part is evaluated subjectively.

Note that both functional and non-functional requirements are important in the development of a software system. However, non-functional requirements, also called quality attributes, play a relevant role during the development of a system, acting as criteria in the selection and/or composition of software architecture, among the various design alternatives.

It should be noted that as systems become larger and more complex, support for nonfunctional requirements increasingly depends on decisions made in software architecture design. It is a view shared by professionals in the field and specifically by the software architecture community.

Non-functional requirements are those that are not directly related to the functionality of a system. The term nonfunctional requirements are also called quality attributes. Non-functional requirements play a major role during the development of a system and can be used as selection criteria in choosing design alternatives, architectural style, and implementation. Disregarding or not properly considering such requirements is costly, as it makes it difficult to correct once the system has been implemented. Suppose, for example, that a decision has been made to modularize the architecture of a system to make it easier to maintain and add new functionality. However, modularizing a system by adding an extra layer can compromise another performance requirement. Therefore,

Non-functional requirements address important quality aspects of software systems. If such requirements are not taken into account, then the software system may be inconsistent and of poor quality, as discussed above. To do so, the earlier the architectural criteria are defined, the sooner the designer can identify the style or combination of styles that is most appropriate to the system under consideration.

When developing a new software system as well as its architecture, software designers or engineers present a set of quality attributes or nonfunctional requirements that the system should support. Examples of these requirements are performance, portability, maintainability, and scalability.

Software architecture should support such requirements. This results from the association between software architecture and non-functional requirements. Important to note that each architectural style (that is, the way system code is organized) supports specific non-functional requirements. The structuring of a system is crucial in supporting a non-functional requirement. For example, using layers allows you to separate the functionality of a system better, making it more modular and easier to maintain.

Consider, for example, the IEEE-Std 830-1993 standard [IEEE 1993], which lists a set of 13 non-functional requirements to be considered in the software requirements specification document. This standard includes but is not limited to performance, reliability, portability, and security requirements.

Although there are a set of proposals, considered complementary, we will focus our attention on a set of requirements that are directly associated with a software system and specifically the software architecture. This set is based on a classification presented by Sommerville, where a distinction is made between external, product, and process requirements [Sommerville 2007].

The next Figure is an adaptation of the proposed Sommerville, where we consider the product requirements associated with the software architecture, and added others not present in the original proposal of Sommerville. It is important to note that Figure 2 shows a subset of non-functional requirements, called product requirements, which are associated with the architecture of a software system. Note that the classification presented in [Sommerville 2007] still considers process requirements and external requirements to be non-functional requirements in addition to product requirements. The figure shows a set of 7 non-functional requirements, some of which are still decomposed.

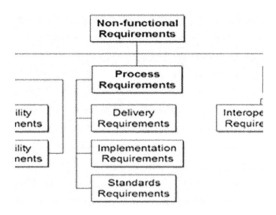

Usability

Usability is one of the quality attributes or non-functional requirements of any interactive system, that is, in which interaction occurs between the system and humans. The notion of usability comes from the fact that any system designed for people to use should be easy to learn and easy to use, making it easy and enjoyable to accomplish any task.

Usability requirements specify both the level of performance and user satisfaction with system usage. Thus, usability can be expressed in terms of:

- Ease of Learning: Associated with the minimum time and effort required to achieve a certain level of system usage performance.

- Ease of use: Related to the speed of task execution and the reduction of errors in system usage.

Usability requirements are collected along with other requirements (data and functional) using some of the requirements elicitation techniques such as interviews or observation. The collection of this data can occur, for example, by checking the user action log when using system functionality.

These usability requirements can be expressed through usability metrics expressed in terms of performance measures. Tyldesley presented a set of criteria that can be used during usability measurement [Tyldesley 1988]. The selection of criteria to be used to measure usability depends on the type of system. Examples of usability measurement criteria are presented in the Figure below.

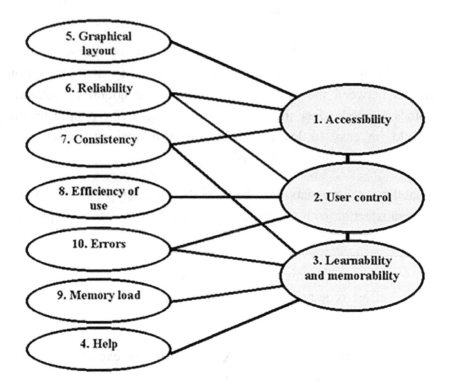

Defining usability goals through metrics is part of the process called usability engineering. In this process, it is also necessary to establish the desired levels of usability. If, for example, the user has difficulty finding the desired functionality in the system and consequently needs to resort to help or express dissatisfaction, then two of the criteria in Figure 3 are considered. The number of times these occurrences are observed is an indicator of the support offered for usability by the system.

Usability is one of the quality attributes of a system and has been increasingly taken into consideration during software development. Usability can be affected by the functional (or application) and presentation components of a system. Even if these components are well designed, usability can still be compromised if the system architecture does not take into account the ease of modification.

other words, software reliability, usually defined in terms of statistical behavior, is the probability that the software will operate as desired over a known time frame. Also, reliability is a software quality attribute, which implies that a system will perform its functions as expected.

Reliability requirements include constraints on software system behavior at runtime. In fact, there is a set of software reliability metrics associated with these requirements. Generally, the failures of a software component are transient, i.e., they occur only for some inputs (stimuli) while the system may continue to operate normally under other circumstances. This distinguishes software from hardware since flaws in the latter are permanent. It is noteworthy that failure is what is observed by users (externally), while defects, originating from within the system, are the drivers of the failures.

It is not so simple to relate the availability of a software system to an existing failure, as it depends on several factors, such as the degree of data corruption due to a software malfunction and restarts time, among others. Examples of metrics used to evaluate software reliability include:

- **Availability:** This is a measure of how available the system would be for use, that is, how available the system would be to perform a service requested by a user. For example, a software system service will have an availability of 999 / 1,000. This means that out of a set of 1,000 service requests, 999 must be fulfilled. This metric is very important in telecommunications systems, for example.

- **Failure Rate:** This is a measure of the frequency at which the system fails to provide a service as expected by the user, i.e., the frequency at which unexpected behavior is likely to be observed. For example, if we have a failure rate of 2 /

1,000, this means that two failures are likely to occur for every 1,000 units of time.

- **Probability of Failure During Operating Phase:** This is a measure of the likelihood that the system will behave unexpectedly when in operation. This metric is of paramount importance in critical systems that require continuous operation.

- **Mean Time to Failure or Mean Time To Failure (MTTF):** This is a measure of the time between observed failures. Note that this metric indicates how long the system will remain operational before a failure occurs.

Any metric that will be used to assess the reliability of a system will depend on how the system is used. Also, note that time is a factor considered in the metrics. It is chosen according to the application. There are software systems that operate continuously, while others operate periodically.

For example, consider a bank ATM. This is an example of a system that operates periodically, that is, an ATM is part of the time in operation, while the rest of the time is idle (although available for use by some bank customer). In the example of a bank ATM, a more appropriate unit of time is the number of transactions. Thus, an example of failure would be the loss of data entered by a user. In this case, the reliability specification could be such a failure occurring every 10,000 transactions.

Software architecture will influence the reliability of a system. The average time to failure or MTTF can be reduced if the replication of critical components occurs. The loss of one of these components fails.

One way to prevent this or to circumvent the loss of a component is by providing a fault-tolerant architecture where a replica of a component takes over the processing of the failed component, thus avoiding any disruption to system operation. Another alternative is to degrade system performance by overloading a component with more requests than it was designed to do. In this way, the quality of the system is degraded, but still, the system continues to function (albeit poorly until corrective action is taken). The measure of reliability can be defined in terms of Mean Time Between Failure (MTBF). This measure is given by:

MTBF = MTTF + MTTR (MTTR or Mean Time To Repair is the average repair time)

Availability measurement can also be described in terms of MTTF and is defined as:

Availability = MTTF x 100% / (MTTF + MTTR)

If we consider these measures, it is important to note that if MTTR is reduced, then system availability and reliability will be higher. This can be achieved architecturally if the separation of interests is considered during the project. Note that the shorter the time to repair the fault, the faster the system will be back up and thus available. This design attribute leads to greater integration as well as easier modifications to the system.

Note that adding redundant components to a software system will result in greater reliability. This redundancy is added in the form of additional checks performed to detect errors before they cause system failures. However, the use of redundant components results in reduced system performance, as discussed below.

Performance

Performance is an important quality attribute for software systems. Consider, for example, a system of a credit card company. In such a system, a designer or software engineer could consider performance requirements to obtain a timely response for card purchase authorization.

Note that performance requirements have a more global impact on the system and are, therefore, among the most important non-functional requirements. However, it is generally difficult to deal with performance requirements and other non-functional requirements as they conflict, as discussed above. At the beginning of the software architecture design activity, it becomes necessary to define which non-functional requirements will be prioritized, given the possibility of conflict between them?

Additionally, performance is important because it affects the usability of a system. If a software system is slow, it certainly reduces the productivity of its users to the point of not meeting their needs. Also, if the software system requires a lot of disk space for storing information, it can be costly to use. For example, if a software system requires a lot of memory to run, it may affect other applications that run in the same environment. In addition, it can run so slowly that the operating system tries to balance memory usage across applications. Overall, the performance requirement can be decomposed in terms of time and space.

The performance requirement restricts the operating speed of a software system. This can be seen in terms of:

Response Requirements

Specify the response time of a software system acceptable to users. In this case, a designer could specify that the system should respond to a user's specific service request within a 2-second interval. For example, at an ATM, after the user inserts the bank's magnetic card in the appropriate place (equipment reader), the system should display a new screen within 2 seconds, requiring the user to enter their current account password. In another situation, the user may be prompted to enter their password and does not do so within 20 seconds, when a timeout occurs and the system returns to the home screen.

Throughput Requirements

These requirements specify how much data should be processed in a given period. An example would be to require the software system to process at least six transactions per second.

Timing Requirements

This type of requirement specifies how quickly the system should collect input data from sensors before other subsequent input data readings overwrite previous data. Thus, for example, it could be specified that the system should read data 5 times per second as a minimum condition.

Space Requirements

In some cases, space requirements may be considered. Here we can refer to main or secondary memory. For example, the main memory for running an application could be considered as a performance requirement since it is related to system behavior at run time.

It is important to note that performance depends on the interaction between the components of a software system and is, therefore, closely associated with the architecture. In this case, the communication mechanisms used by the components of a system influence the performance obtained. As we saw earlier, performance is related to other nonfunctional requirements. For example, reliability improves with the use of redundant components. However, the performance is very compromised, implying its reduction.

Portability

Portability can be defined as the ease with which software can be transferred from one computer system or environment to another. In other words, the software is said to be portable if it can be run in different environments. Note that the term environment may refer to both the hardware platform and a software environment, such as a specific operating system.

Generally speaking, portability refers to the ability to run a system on different platforms. It is important to note that as the cost ratio between software and hardware increases, portability becomes increasingly important. Additionally, we can have component portability and system portability. The latter situation can be seen as a special case of reusability. Software reuse occurs when the entire software system is reused, implementing it in different computer systems.

The portability of a software component or system is proportional to the amount of effort it takes to function in a new environment. If less effort is required compared to development work, then the system is said to be portable.

Two relevant aspects of program portability are transfer and adaptation. Transfer is the movement of component (program code and associated data) from one environment to another. Adaptation encompasses the modifications required to make the program run in a new environment.

It should be noted that the environment in which a software system operates is usually composed of hardware, operating system, input, and output system (I / O) as well as the application. A general approach that could be taken to obtain a portable system would be to try to separate the external environment-dependent parts of the system into a portability layer or interface, as illustrated in Figure below.

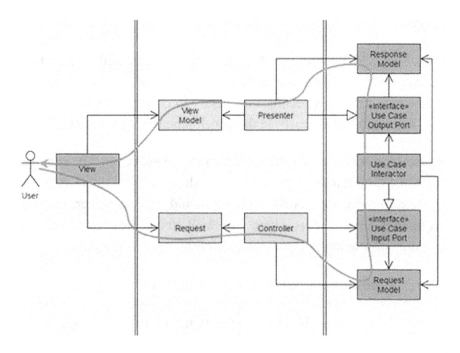

The portability interface shown in the figure above can be glimpsed and projected as a set of abstract data types or objects, which would encapsulate unportable elements by seeking to hide features of the application software. Thus, when the software system changes hardware or operating system, only the portability interface would need to be changed. Some portability issues generally arise due to the adoption of different conventions for representing information on different machine architectures, i.e., different hardware.

Reusability

A feature of engineering is to make use of existing designs to reuse already developed components to minimize the strain on new designs. This way, components that have already been developed and tested can be reused. Consider the high levels of reusability we find in both the auto and electronics industries. In the car industry, for example, an engine is usually reused from one car model to another.

In Software Engineering, as the pressure to reduce software system development and maintenance costs, as well as high-quality systems, increases, it becomes necessary to consider reusability as a non-functional requirement in the development of new systems.

Reuse can be viewed from different perspectives. It can be component-oriented, process-oriented, or domain-specific knowledge oriented. Note that we could still consider reusing requirements. However, here we will focus our attention on component-oriented reuse. Examples of this type of reuse are:

- **Application:** The entire application could be reused.

- **Subsystems:** The main subsystems of an application could be reused.

- **Objects or Modules:** Components of a system, encompassing a set of functions, can be reused.

- **Functions:** Software components that implement a single function (such as a math function) can be reused.

Two types of reuse that we are most interested in are the reuse of subsystems and objects or components, which we will simply call component reuse. This type of reuse not only involves code but also encompasses the associated architecture and design.

It is important to note that we can gain by reusing both designs and architectures. This minimizes development efforts and requires fewer changes or adaptations. In fact, when you have to keep in mind that you need to support easy modification, we indirectly get reusable components.

Thus, the reusability requirement may involve the architecture of a software system or components thereof. What will determine how easy it will be to get reusable components is the interdependence or coupling between the components? For example, a component library that offers a set of features already implemented and tested offers the user (developer) a valuable feature by simply incorporating these components into their code and accessing their functionality through their interface.

Safety

In a software system, this non-functional requirement characterizes the security that unauthorized system access and associated data will not be allowed. Therefore, the integrity of the system against intentional attacks or accidents is ensured. Thus, security is viewed as the probability that the threat of some kind will be repelled.

In addition, as software systems become distributed and connected to external networks, security requirements become increasingly important. Examples of security requirements are:

- Only persons who have been authenticated by an access and authentication control component will be able to view information as confidentiality allows such access only to authorized persons.

- Only the system administrator can change system access permissions.

- All system data should be backed up every 24 hours, and these copies should be stored in a secure location, preferably in a location other than where the system is located.

- All external communications between the system data server and clients must be encrypted.

Safety requirements are essential in critical systems, such as aircraft flight control systems, as it is impossible to rely on such a system if it is unsafe. Thus it can be said that all critical systems have security requirements associated with them. Non-functional safety requirements involve different aspects.

It is also important to consider the different emphases found for safety:

- **Availability:** Refers to ensuring the system against any interruption of service.

- **Integrity:** The focus on integrity occurs primarily in commercial systems, where it is sought to ensure that unauthorized access or updates occur.

- **Confidentiality:** The emphasis here is not to allow unauthorized disclosure of information.

- **Operational Safety:** Refers to the phase considered for the system in use.

Note that, to satisfy the non-functional quality security requirement in a software system, some methods may be employed. These methods can be seen as a refinement of the goal of providing security to a software system. As examples of these methods, we can consider:

Identification

Identifies the username, telling the system which is using it.

Authentication

It aims to ensure that users are, in fact, who they claim to be. To do so, they do an identity test. This method involves some aspects such as:

- **Type of protocol used:** This requires password operation.

- **Number of Authentications:** May require a single password or multiple passwords or procedures. For example, some banks already use multiple passwords during the authentication operation.

- **Stakeholders:** This may involve the authentication of a stakeholder (client) or both parties (client and system).

Access Time

It seeks to limit system access time to reduce any kind of threat.

Security Audit

It aims to enable authorized personnel to monitor the system and selectively track important events.

Alarm

This operation is intended to prevent potentially suspicious access to vital information or system data by notifying such access to system security supervision or appropriate authorities.

It is important to note that the architecture of a software system must take these aspects into account to meet security requirements. However, the type of system will determine which factors need to be taken into account. Thus, there may be the insertion of specific safety components as well as their connection with other functional components.

The elicitation of functional and non-functional requirements is a fundamental step in the development of software systems. Input elements of this elicitation process include the main influencers of the system, involving designer, architect, and users.

Coupled with this, the experience of the software architect is of great importance. As a result of this process, there is a set of functional requirements supporting system functionality and a list of non-functional requirements supporting software architecture. It should be noted that when analyzing candidate architectures for a software system, an architect or software engineer considers non-functional requirements as one of the main criteria for their analysis.

Finally, it is important to note that full coverage of all possible non-functional requirements is beyond the scope of this chapter. To do so, the reader may refer to the book entitled NonFunctional Requirements in Software Engineering by L. Chung, E. Yu, and J. Mylopoulos. However, a subset of the most prominent non-functional requirements was presented. These requirements serve as a rule, as a criterion for architectural analysis aiming at defining the software architecture of a system.

Chapter Six

Usability and Software Architecture

Since the middle of the last century, the interaction between people and computers (HCI, Human-Computer Interaction) has become an area of study. The objective is to provide theoretical, methodological and practical bases for the design and evaluation of interactive products that can be used efficiently, effectively, safely and satisfactorily.

The technological increase revolutionized the ways of developing computer systems, which led to the emergence of information architecture (from now on AI). The objective of this area of knowledge within software development focused (between 60 and 200) on determining the functionality of the product and specifying how users would find the information through interactive interfaces. Therefore, its main characteristics are the organization of information, the forms of navigation, the labeling system (names of categories and general and specific classes that group information content), and the functionality of search systems.

As of 2010, the trend in software development must not only be easy to use but must also be innovative and focused on creating unique experiences. The limitations of the traditional approaches to the design of interactive interfaces lie mainly in the fact of making the user interfaces easy to use, ignoring variables as important as emotional behavior.

At present, the development and use of technologies are increasingly varied and widespread, growing at an accelerated pace and reaching extraordinary levels. This has resulted in the expansion of dissimilar projects for the computerization of society, thereby facilitating the performance of the daily tasks of citizens. From this point of view, the main element in the development and acceptance of new technologies will be the adaptation of them to the way of thinking of users. Therefore, the ultimate goal, pursued by large industries dedicated to software development, is to design simpler interactive products, more focused on human needs and that help increase the effectiveness and satisfaction of people.

An interactive program is one that needs a continuous exchange with the user to run. In this chapter, we refer to interactive software products, which facilitate social interaction through the application of friendly and easy-to-use interfaces. This interactivity and its impact on society are studied through the human-machine interaction discipline, whose main objective is to use computers to respond to the needs of people interactively. It is a term that is widely applied in the sciences of communication, computer science, multimedia design, and industrial design.

This makes the exchange with the user one of the most significant elements of any software, and it is basically the interface, which provides this dialog to allow the user to access the resources of the computer. The user interface will largely determine the perception and impression that it has of the application. People do not use interactive systems, but use the interfaces that provide them, therefore, a very important part of the success or failure of an interactive application depends on that interface.

Many institutions and experts that produce software attach more importance to functionalities and very little in the way users interact. They ignore the interest in those users who experiment with the software interaction processes. This leads to the fact that a product is often unusable despite its functional quality due to difficulties in its exploitation.

In the investigation of generalizable solutions, in recent years, the concept of user experience (UX) or design of user experiences (DUX) has been disseminated, a Paraguayan concept under which different disciplines and professional roles are integrated to get users to experience emotions when interacting with products.

In software development, usability is recognized as a quality attribute in the success of a product to ensure the required usability levels empirically. However, there are few processes and professionals that apply or take into account techniques and procedures to achieve this attribute and less those that focus on DUX of their interactive systems.

The user experience represents a change in the concept of usability, as the objective is not reduced to improve user performance in the interaction between effectiveness, efficiency, and ease of learning, but tries to solve the strategic problem of the usefulness of the product and the psychological problem of pleasure and fun of its use.

To better understand the aspects of AI and DUX, in the software development process, this technical report is presented to know these key concepts and their close relationship with the development stages of a software product. Based on the diversity of authors dealing with the topic of AI and DXU, the most cited definitions and their relationship with the term user experience were identified.

The activities that can be carried out in each phase of product development are also explained. Identifying the largest number of requirements and needs of the user through these techniques, makes users feel directly involved and thus obtain more information. These activities and techniques constitute a working instrument for the information architect, most responsible for identifying and organizing the information and satisfying the interaction needs that the user expects to find in the product.

Information Architecture Definitions

The term information architecture was coined by (Wurman, 1975) in the second half of the 70s and defined as "the study of the organization of information to allow the user to find their way of navigation towards knowledge and knowledge. understanding of information ", cited by (Resmini and Rosati, 2012, p. 2)

In the evolution of the definition of AI, (Rosenfeld and Morville, 2006, p. 26) they extrapolated the concept to the field of web application development, stating the discipline as

The art and science of shaping information products and experiences to support usability and findability [the art and science of structuring and classifying websites and intranets to help users find and manage information].

Information architecture is the discipline in charge of arranging the formal and content elements that make up a website. He comments that the informative content and the design must have the required quality to achieve full user satisfaction. The implementation of coherent information architecture cannot be achieved without incorporating the elements that determine the best use of the site. At this point, usability acquires particular relevance.

Information architecture is not the only component of the design of digital information spaces. It must also work with information visualization, evaluation, usability, human-machine interaction, and advanced programming techniques, all of them integrated and highly

112

interrelated under the term "information design." In addition, it states that it is almost impossible to separate the aspects of design, architecture, and usability in a digital document system.

In software applications, (Folmer and Bosch, 2018) study this fact and conclude that design at the architecture level has a great influence on the usability of the system. From the same line of practical research work, experts agree that the graphic interface design of a product is an element of importance for users in their first interaction with a computer application, but also its usability depends on the structuring and organization of the content shown. They also agree that visuality is one of the fundamental characteristics of AI results; therefore, they are closely complemented. In many software development teams, the performance of a designer's activities begins basically after the information architecture has been approved.

The information architecture is also defined as the art and science of structuring and organizing information environments to help people effectively fulfill their information needs [the art and science of organizing information spaces to help users meet their information needs].

In AI, there are two important aspects to take into account, first, the recovery of information, whose main objective is to facilitate the user to reach the content that indicates the structured categories. This is achieved by, on the one hand, enabling the user to find information, design, and definition of indexes, classifications, taxonomies, and information retrieval systems or search systems on the website and on the other hand, enabling each element of information to be found (description through metadata and search engine optimization). This second case is known as "findability.", find or visibility. The second aspect is the design at the conceptual level, the AI's own techniques, within the life cycle of the development of a website, are located in conceptual design phases. The visual design phases are, they are characterized by techniques of Usability Engineering, Interface Design and Information Design.

Also highlighting the importance of the information architect, we can say that an information architect does not necessarily have to be a specialist in information sciences or in other disciplines related to software development. However, the task of the information architect also includes the constant review of the flows linked to the work process of the development team, as well as the coordination between the different disciplines that make up the team (systems analysts, designers, communicators, programmers, among others).

In the last two decades, with the advent of the Internet, the use of AI has rapidly spread, which is considered a multidisciplinary and relatively young subject. There has also been an explosion of information architects who, in their work, mix three major fields: technology, graphic design, and journalism/writing. However, the information architect must also have basic knowledge of Information Sciences, Communication Sciences, Engineering in usability, Marketing, Informatics, Psychology and Sociology.

After the contribution of (Wurman, 1975), others took their definitions and began to broaden the AI horizon, making the definition of their scope of action more accurate. (Morville, 2004) assumes the ideas of this author in his definitions and states that AI is defined through three sentences:

- The combination of organization, labeling, and navigation schemes within an information system.

- The structural design of an information space to facilitate the completion of tasks and intuitive access to content.

- The art and science of structuring and classifying websites and intranets, to help people find and manage information.

From this definition, (Wurman, 1975) and (Morville, 2004) establishes the specific tasks that an information architect performs:

- Clarify the mission and vision of the site, balancing the needs of the organization that drives it and the needs of its audiences.

- Determine what content and functionality the site should contain.

- Specify how users will search the site for information by defining their organization, navigation, tagging, and search systems.

- Project how the site will adapt to change and growth over time.

Traditionally, in the development of software products, the information architecture was applied to organize content, find and manage information that meets the basic knowledge needs of users. The accelerated advance of technologies has led to the evolution of this concept through the development of interactive products between man and computers. This interactivity makes it possible to identify the user's rational behavior in their skills and knowledge, but their emotional behavior was not yet widely considered.

From a social approach, the user's emotional behavior is a key element in the acceptance and use of the products. Not only do computer applications require the organization of content and meet cognitive demands, but they also influence user training, their expertise to assimilate and work with information technologies, their tastes, preferences, education, environment or social and labor in which it develops, values, feelings, idiosyncrasy, culture, among others. This new approach to the development of interactive products, mainly used to find more integrative and inclusive design solutions in the professional web development environment, is known as the user experience (from now on UX).

User Experience Genesis and Definitions

The UX is a concept that focuses directly on the emotions that the user experiences when interacting with software products. In this regard, experts explain that the user's emotional behavior is the result of three different factors: "the emotions evoked by the product during the interaction, the mood of the user and the feelings pre-associated by the user to the product." In this sense, it is necessary to recognize that the traditional approach to the design of interactive products on the web has limitations because its vision of the phenomenon is based on the side of the media, tools, and technologies used.

In addition, experts continue to say that one of the contributions of the UX is its concept function to integrate the different disciplines and professional roles involved in the design of interactive products such as usability engineering, the architecture of the information, graphic design, interaction design, information design, among others.

The UX represents a change in the concept of usability itself, since the objective is not reduced to improve user performance in the interaction between efficiency, efficiency, and ease of learning, but tries to solve the strategic problem of the usefulness of the product and the psychological problem of pleasure and fun of its use (D'Hertefelt, 2000).

The genesis of this concept is in the field of Marketing, as it considers (Kankainen, 2002). This is due to its link with the concept of brand experience "Claim to establish a family and consistent relationship between consumer and brand." In the context of marketing, a UX-focused approach would involve not only analyzing the factors that influence the acquisition or choice of a particular product but also analyzing how consumers use the product and the experience resulting from its use. Being a concept of recent application in the field of design, it is necessary to appreciate different definitions and proposed models, which allow an approach to what is understood by the UX. Integrated from three levels, (Dillon, 2001) defines the UX: action, what does the user do; the result, what does the user get; and emotion, what the user feels. This approach breaks down the causative phenomenon (interaction) into two levels, action and result, and only interested in the user's emotional behavior in the resulting experience.

(Arhippainen and Tähti, 2003) from Linköping University in Sweden define the UX as the user experience when interacting with a product in particular conditions. They also highlight the emotions and expectations of the user and their relationship with other people and the context of use.

For its part, (FatDUX Group, 2013) defines the user experience as the sum of a series of interactions. It is a term for the level of total user satisfaction when using your product or system. It represents the perception left in someone's mind after a series of interactions between people, devices, and events - or a combination of interactions.

From an emotional vision, experts also focus on it, stating that the user experience encompasses the set of factors and elements that determine the satisfactory interaction of the user with an

117

environment or device and are capable of generating a set of positive emotions in it about the site and its use.

For some experts, the UX "is the feeling, emotional response, assessment, and satisfaction of the user regarding a product, the result of the phenomenon of interaction with the product, and the interaction with its provider." We can describe that the UX is the process of different disciplines and professional roles involved in the design of interactive products, usability engineering, information architecture, graphic design, interaction design are integrated, information design, etc.

(Nielsen Norman Group, 2003, p.1-2) defines the UX as: "Integrative concept of all aspects of the interaction between the end-user and the company, its services, and products." The analysis of the experience stands out of interaction not only as an interactive phenomenon between user and product but also between user and supplier.

Also, the first requirement for an exemplary UX is to meet the exact needs of the customer. Then come the simplicity and elegance that generate easy-to-use products. The true user experience goes far beyond giving customers what they say they want or providing a checklist. To achieve high-quality UX in a company's offer, there must be a seamless merger of the services of multiple disciplines, including engineering, marketing, graphic and industrial design, and interface design (Nielsen Norman Group, 2003).

(Morville, 2004) presents "the facets of the UX," which are represented with a hexagon whose set gives rise to a diagram that has popularly been called "The Morville panel." The most important conclusion of this approach is the UX, seen as the integration of various disciplines and qualities. The UX is composed of six elements:

A. Useful: it can be understood as the utility that the site has for the user, the ability to respond to their needs.

B. Usable: related to ease of use, it depends closely on the application of the concepts of the science of interaction person computer.

C. Desirable: closely related to emotional design. A software is desirable as a product of efficiency in harmony with the image, graphics, and brand management.

D. Findable: refers to the ability of a site to be navigable. Users should be able to find the elements that will respond to their needs.

E. Accessible: for a site, it will be important to try to guarantee access to the greatest number of people in the greatest number of contexts.

F. Credible: indicates the need to show the elements that expose a credible and reliable portal to users.

(Garrett, 2011) divides decisions into four planes, to be taken in the DX. In addition, strategies are used, which consists of the stage in which the basis of the project is specified. It is about clearly establishing what your managers and users expect from the site.

- Scope: includes the functions and characteristics of the site.

- Structure: these are the so-called blueprints or site plans that define the relationship between the various web pages, navigation structures, and their flows, etc.

- Skeleton: are the so-called wireframes or schemes where the various elements that make up the interface and the relationship between these are located: menus, buttons, images, paragraphs, etc.

- Surface: is the visual design of the elements that comprise the pages of the site.

The design of UX goes beyond pursuing the ease of use in products to achieve innovative proposals and focused on creating experiences unique. It does not constitute a closed and defined discipline, but an open and multidisciplinary work approach. The projections must be focused so that users experience pleasure when interacting with the systems, be framed in that the functional criteria (which are obvious) are not enough, so an emotional dimension of the use and enjoyment of an interactive application must be achieved, by the medium of a focus on emotional design.

Conceptual Analysis Between Information Architecture and User Experience

Based on the above definitions of these two terms, an analysis of meaning and syntax was performed on the contents of the definitions described. For both analyses, all the definitions in the field were introduced in a bibliographic manager (endnote): abstract. Then, the keywords were extracted, which contain a logical meaning, described in the content of the concepts in the field: keywords. Subsequently, with the tool itself, a filter is made to count attributes, which are the characteristics described in the definitions through the keywords), with the bibliographic subject option by the keywords indicator. The system returns those words found and written in the same way-syntax and the number of times they match. Subsequently, an analysis is carried out on the content of the definitions by the meaning they contain, looking for those terms that explain the same semantic idea.

For the definitions corresponding to the concept of AI, the following stand out as main terms: web browsing, information structure, information organization, and classification of information. All authors agree that the information architecture is more focused on the organization of content and classification of information for products with a web interface, seeking user interactivity. It also uses activities/techniques focused on the user to meet their information needs and organize the contents based on it.

Among the attributes with semantic coincidence stand out: information structure, content structure, manage information, manage information, manage information, space design, space organization, information design, visualization, visual quality, visibility, taxonomies, indexes, metadata.

On the other hand, in the definitions of UX, the terms that most coincide in the syntactic structure are a pleasure, interaction, usability, software, the user. They also relate other attributes that describe the organization of information content, satisfaction, emotions, among others. With ideas of similar meanings, the words: pleasure, pleasant, happiness, desirable, sensations, feeling; interaction, interactivity, interaction design; structure, information design, skeleton, surface, information architecture, graphic design; emotion, emotional behavior, emotional response.

Usability

Among the most recognized and cited authors on this subject are (Nielsen, 2001) and (Krug, 2006), who addresses the definition of usability in close connection with AI. Hence, they consider that usability appears as a natural conclusion of the information architecture process. These ideas are based on the fact that the user of a website does not want to think about how to use an interface, but only use it for the purposes that led him to visit it. Therefore, everything that is presented on the screen must be generated with that idea in mind.

(Nielsen, 1999) states that usability is a quality attribute that determines how easy the interfaces are to use, while (Krug, 2013) indicates that screens should avoid making the user think. This means that as much as humanly possible when looking at a web page, it should be self-evident, obvious, and self-explanatory. It should be possible to "understand" it, what it is and how it is used, without making efforts to think about it.

The quality of use of an interactive product is recognized as usability. The term is really an anglicism that means ease of use. It refers to the degree of effectiveness, efficiency, and satisfaction with which specific users can achieve specific objectives in specific contexts of use (International Standard Organization, 1994).

User Experience and Information Architecture in the Software Development Process

From the bibliographic review carried out in the previous paragraphs, this section coincides with the idea that the user experience is an umbrella term under that the information architecture is included. It is closely linked with different disciplines in which various professional roles are developed (information architects, designers, systems analysts, computer scientists, communicators, psychologists, among others).

The common point in both concepts is the user as the most important element during software development. The two terms have the main objective to satisfy the needs of the user, one in an organized way through the information contents and the other based on the emotions they experience when interacting with the software.

They also integrate other essential components in achieving the final realization of the software and user satisfaction when interacting with them.

In addition, it agrees with the criteria of (Nielsen Norman Group, 2003) when they state that to ensure that software meets the required levels of usability empirically, the designer needs a methodology, techniques, and procedures designed for this purpose. In this sense, some proposals guide this process as a methodological framework known as user-centered design (User-Centered Design), adapting it to the characteristics of software development.

The user-centered design is characterized by assuming that the entire process of developing a software product is aimed at the user, their needs, characteristics, and objectives. Focusing the design on its users, contrary to focusing on technological possibilities or on the designers themselves, implies involving them from the beginning in the product development process. It means to know how they are, what they need, what they use them for, test the software with end-users, investigate how they react to the design, how is their experience of use, and always innovate to improve the user experience.

However, the integration of the user, as the main element in the development of software, goes beyond satisfying their emotions through the interpretation of others, also means allowing them to manifest themselves directly in the interaction with the product, your tastes, and usefulness. The user-centered design also includes co-designer himself, and this manifests from the identification of their needs to the implementation of the product.

When performing tests on non-functional prototypes (architectural models) and functional prototypes (designed), using various techniques; The architect obtains new visual and interactive

123

elements that the user manifests during the tests. These are used to improve the interactive and visual design, which manifests itself in better functioning of the product when it is implemented. Therefore, the user himself before having the finished product acts as a co-designer in software development.

These characteristics correspond exactly with the focus of this work, which defends the participation of the user with his experience from the beginning and until the end of the development of applications of human-machine interaction. If you take into account the type of audience, community, group of people, users in question, to which a software product is aimed, as well as your experience to handle a computer application, AI will have the expected quality and usability levels required.

The user-centered design during software production is of vital importance since its practices involve optimizing the ease of use of processes, breaking technological barriers for people with disabilities, organizing information according to the mental model of the target audience, evaluate the application with real users and solve usability errors. In addition, collaborating in the design of the application interface, checking to what extent this design adapts to potential users, checking the operation on different platforms, as well as performing different tests that contribute to validate the design of this experience, contributes to creating a pleasant emotional state in the interaction with the systems.

Activities and Techniques of AI and DXU in Software Development

For the development of software, the architectural proposal based on the user experience is ideal, as this allows you to meet your information needs when interacting with the product and guarantees an important part of the success of its use. The manufacture of a software product goes through several phases, according to the development methodology used. These stages have AI incorporated into the design of the application. To make quality AI, techniques are applied at the required stages of the production process. These techniques are adapted to each specific project, depending on the product that is developed.

In general, the software life cycle transits through four fundamental phases: business model, requirements, analysis and design, implementation, and testing. Seen from the managerial point of view, the information architect organizes his activities focused on each stage. The requirements correspond to the planning activities, in the design with the organization activities, the implementation with the execution, and in the test with the control of the product. For both approaches, the bulk of activities related to the information architecture is concentrated in the requirements, design, and part of the product tests stage.

Each stage in the AI implies a group of tasks that seek a more realistic approach to user expectations. These tasks are accompanied by techniques that allow more information to be obtained and computer solutions with greater quality and use. These techniques can be applied in combination at different times in the software development process, as required.

The information architect has high participation in the software development process since it is present in 75% of its execution (planning, organization, and control). This is manifested in the activities and tasks that you must perform during the software development cycle. However, it is at the beginning of the project where the greatest activities to carry out to obtain information lie.

The information architect should always take into account aspects such as:

- The goals and needs of the users

- The goals of the business or organization

- Technological limitations

- Content Limitations

- Project Limitations

Developing a good software design focused on the user experience brings great benefits for everyone involved in the process: the user to whom it is intended and the members of the work team. The user allows you to understand and move through large amounts of information, search, and find the information they need simply, not having to think and experience emotions when interacting with the product.

The creators (which includes the entire development team-project managers, analysts, information architects, programmers, designers, among others), allow them to generate structures that support the change and growth of the product over time. Ensure the consistency and location of the information. Create intuitive navigation systems and ensure a large percentage of the usability of the software.

Other general techniques can also be applied at any stage, such as study of the cultural environment in which users develop (language, country, traditions, level of education, cultural level, etc.), study of language used by users (vulgar, scientific, colloquial, etc.), compendium of documents they use, collection of words or words of use from documents and language studies, and frequency analysis of terms within the documentation (quantitative method).

Finally, we can see that:

- The information architecture and the user experience are two interrelated concepts that, when applied in an integrated way in software development, guarantee a high percentage of product usability.

- The user is considered as the fundamental element of success in the development of software. Only the efficient, effective, and satisfactory use of the system will justify the investment in money, time, and development personnel.

- AI and UX can be applied in the development of any software product: website, multimedia, information systems, management system, search engines, or others.

- The DUX is aimed at creating direct, simple, and easy-to-use interfaces, in addition, innovative and pleasant, imposing a new approach to software development that involves inserting its practices to improve products.

- The active participation of the users, in a well-designed system, will make them feel skilled, proficient, and will understand it naturally, achieving the goals that led them to use it.

- The information architect plays a fundamental role in the software development process since it avoids mistakes in structure, nomenclature, navigation.

- The use of techniques to obtain information at each stage of the process helps to define better an architecture design designed in the user experience, allows relating the technical tasks of software engineering with the creative characteristics of the DUX.

Chapter Seven

Domain-Driven Design
In Clean Architecture

What is the domain? Thematic area or field to which a user applies software.

What is the domain model? It represents the terminology and key concepts of the problem domain. It identifies the relationships between the entities included within the scope of the problem domain, identifies their attributes, and provides a structural vision of the domain.

Domain-driven design is an approach to software development defined by Eric Evans in his book Domain-driven design: Tackling Complexity in the Heart of Software, which focuses on a rich, expressive, and constantly evolving model to solve domain mastery problems. a semantic form

A Common Language (Ubiquitous Language)

One of the biggest problems that arise during the development of software projects is communication between developers and domain experts.

Domain experts have extensive knowledge about the domain; on the contrary, their knowledge of the technical terminology used in software development is quite limited. On the other hand, the developers understand and handle the technical terminology;

however, usually, our knowledge about the problem domain is quite limited. Either because we have never faced a problem within that domain or if we have done so, most likely it was from a different perspective or environment, since companies in the same sector can approach their problems in a totally different way. This difference in languages and knowledge usually gives rise to situations in which domain experts describe confusingly and ambiguously what they expect from the system.

In projects where there is no common language, we are forced to carry out a translation process to communicate with the domain experts. In turn, domain experts have to perform a translation process in the opposite direction to communicate with developers. Often the developers themselves are forced to do translations when we communicate with other developers.

Each time a translation is done, concepts are misunderstood and confused, causing different team members to understand concepts differently, and even worse, without being aware of it. These misinterpretations make the software contain inconsistencies and contradictions within the code that will cause errors in the system.

All these problems during the communication process between team members mean that, on the one hand, we lose opportunities to gain a deeper knowledge of the domain and, on the other hand, is even more important, the terminology used for communication is not reflected in the software.

To be able to generate a common language, developers have to obtain the necessary knowledge of the domain, while domain experts must be an active part of software development. So that both the domain of the problem, as the elements of the software design (classes, relationships, etc.) are part of the common language and are understood by developers and domain experts, since experts know the domain in detail, they must oppose changes in the model that are not suitable for the correct transmission of knowledge included in the domain, with developers being the ones who should control possible ambiguities and inconsistencies that hinder the design of the system.

The process to reach a common language is iterative, so we must exercise the language and polish it through its use both in diagrams, as in writing, and especially in verbal communication. This will make the language evolve and change. These changes must be reflected in the code, so we must refactor that code to reflect the changes that occur in the language.

To carry out the task of linking domain knowledge to the implementation of the model, we have different elements. We will describe the elements that are used to model operations that belong to a specific object (entities and value objects) and the elements that represent activities or actions that conceptually belong to more than one object.

Entities

The entities are objects of the model that are characterized by having an identity in the system; the attributes they contain are not their main characteristic. They represent concepts with an identity that is maintained over time, and that is also often maintained under different representations of the entity. They must be able to be distinguished from other objects even if they have the same attributes. They have to be considered equal to other objects, even when their attributes differ.

For example, let's imagine a Person object with a first and last name as attributes of a class in a system where two objects representing two different people with the same first and last names should be considered different.

As we can see, in this case, we cannot describe the person object primarily by its attributes. Still, we must assign it an identity that is maintained for any representation of that person. If our system works only with USA nationals, we could consider the DNI as an identity. Still, if we manage people of any nationality, we may have to generate this ID within our system (Many countries do not have a national identity document). It should be noted that in one system, a person can be considered an entity, while in another system where we do not need to identify a person by their identity, it may not be.

The identity has to be declared in such a way that we can track the entity effectively. Attributes, responsibilities, and relationships must be defined in relation to the identity that the entity represents rather than in the attributes that compose it.

As we can see, the fact that we need to identify and distinguish different objects throughout their life cycle makes the complexity to handle and design them much greater than that of those who do not need it. For this reason, we must use entities only for objects that really require it, which has two important advantages. On the one hand, we will not include unnecessary complexity in objects that do not need to be identified. On the other hand, by reducing the number of entities in the system, we will be able to identify them quickly.

Value Objects

Unlike entities, value objects represent concepts that have no identity. They simply describe features. Therefore we are only interested in its attributes.

The value objects represent elements of the model that are described by WHAT they are, and not by WHO or WHAT they are.

Take, for example, a Color object represented by its RGB composition (Red, Green, and Blue). If we had two objects representing the same color, we could use any of them since we are interested in what color it is by its attributes, not by which instance we are using. Other examples of value objects could be String or Integer since we don't care what "C" or "3" we are using. Although these examples are simple, value objects do not have to be.

This entails a series of differences when modeling value objects with respect to entities. The value objects are usually modeled as immutable. They are less complex to design since we can use them and discard them as we are interested because we do not have to worry about the instance we are using (as long as their attributes are correct).

Both entities and value objects represent concepts, so they are usually named with nouns.

In the next part of this chapter, we will describe in detail what another of the fundamental parts of domain-driven design, services, and how to isolate the details of the domain layer from the rest of the system, so stay tuned with your reading!

The Domain Layer

In the first part of this chapter, we discussed one of the most important concepts in domain-driven design, the Ubiquitous language. We also began to describe some of the basic elements to model the domain of the software, such as Entities and Value Objects. In this section, we will define what they are and what types of services exist, and we will end up describing how to isolate the domain layer from the rest of the system.

Services

Services represent operations, actions, or activities that do not conceptually belong to any specific domain object. Services have neither their own status nor a meaning beyond the action that defines them.

Unlike entities and value objects, services are defined in terms of what they can do for a client and therefore tend to be named as verbs. The verbs used to name the services must belong to the ubiquitous language, or be introduced in the case they are not yet. When implementing both its parameters and results must be objects belonging to the domain.

A service must fulfill three main characteristics:

1. The operation that defines it is related to a domain concept, but it is not natural to model it as an entity or a value object.

2. Its interface is specified using other elements of the domain model.

3. The operation has no status, so any customer could use any instance of the service without taking into account the operations that have been performed previously in that instance.

We can divide the services into three different types according to their relationship with the core of the domain.

133

Domain Services

They are responsible for the more specific behavior of the domain, that is, they perform actions that do not depend on the specific application that we are developing, but that belongs to the most internal part of the domain, and that could make sense in other applications belonging to the same domain. For example, create a user, update the details of a client, etc.

Application Services

They are responsible for the main flow of the application; that is, they are the use cases of our application. They are the visible part outside the domain of our system, so they are the point of entry-exit to interact with the internal functionality of the domain. Its function is to coordinate entities, value objects, domain services, and infrastructure services to act. For example, make a payment, add a product to the shopping cart, make a transfer to another account, etc. (If you are familiar with "Clean Architecture" the application services would be equivalent to the "Interactors")

Infrastructure Services

They declare behavior that does not really belong to the domain of the application but that we must be able to perform as part of it. For example, send a confirmation email after making a payment, logging transactions, etc.

Different applications have different levels of complexity in their domains, and that can make differentiating between domain and application services not always trivial. As a general idea, we could consider that if, after receiving an order, the system needs to perform several steps, the coordination of these steps would be carried out in application service. If, on the other hand, we receive a simple order that is related to a domain concept, this behavior should probably be modeled as a domain service.

To clarify the difference between the different services and their responsibilities, let's give the example of an application service that, given some products in the shopping cart, makes the payment. We will name our application service as MakePaymentService.

MakePaymentService will have to validate the user, apply discounts, verify that we have stock products available, make a call to an external payment service, notify the parcel delivery service, send a confirmation email to the user, etc.

The responsibility of MakePaymentService is the coordination of the flow to make a payment. On the other hand, to act upon validating the user, we would use a ValidateUserService that would be a domain service, and that would have the responsibility of validating that the user is valid, since a priori it is a simple order that is related to a domain concept. Instead, for the action of sending a confirmation email to the user, we would use SendEmailService which in this case would be an infrastructure service, since it is an action that our domain must be able to perform but does not belong to it. Therefore, it would be specified in our domain as an interface (in the case of Java), which, as we will see below, would be implemented within another layer of our system (infrastructure).

Layered Architecture

A software system is made up of many parts, of which the part that solves problems for the domain is a small portion, although its importance is disproportionate to its size.

To be able to work with the domain without getting lost in other details present in the software, we need to decouple domain objects from other system functions. We will have to isolate our domain from the rest of the system to avoid confusing concepts belonging to the domain with concepts that are only related to the technology used.

We can use any of the many architectures that exist to isolate the different parts of the system. Still, the option we choose should divide our system into at least four layers: presentation, application, domain, and infrastructure.

Presentation
Layer responsible for displaying information to the user and interpreting user input events. It should be noted that the user can be a human being or another system that communicates with ours.

Application
Layer that declares the functionalities that the software has to carry out and orchestrates the domain objects to solve the different problems. This layer does not contain business rules or knowledge; it only coordinates and delegates the work to the collaboration of the domain objects that are in the next layer.

Domain
The layer where domain concepts and business rules are located. It is the most important layer of the system, and it really adds value and solves the problems for which a certain software is created.

Infrastructure
Layer that provides the implementations that support the layers defined above. Here most of the technical decisions adopted for a system are encapsulated, for example, the sending of the confirmation email after payment, persistence for the domain, communication with other systems, etc.

The process of obtaining knowledge and building software is complex and tedious. It is an iterative process, in which we will discover new concepts and abstractions that we will have to capture in the code and in the language used to communicate.

On many occasions, we will discover how a deeper knowledge of the domain and its inclusion in the codebase will make parts of the system that a priori seemed complex or in which we had difficulties to model or design become trivial. Giving way to the creation of expressive, semantic software, easy to understand, manage, and modify.

Conclusion

Finally, by simply putting the lessons of this book, we can say, software architecture defines how a system works and how new modules can be built intuitively. If we could make a comparison with traditional architecture, it would be like this: when we look at the blueprint of a building, we can assume what kind of building is being designed, isn't it?

Thus, when asking ourselves what software architecture is, we must be able to intuit what kind of application will be built. Designing a hospital management application is not the same as developing an ATM system. Each has a different architecture project.

That is, consider that the software architecture design translates into the very structure of folders and packages - as in the case of Java - or any language that is used that helps express the intent of the system itself, without telling exactly how it is done.

We can also talk about "clean architectures" that have several common goals:

1. They are independent of frameworks;

2. Testable. Based on codes that can be tested;

3. Independent of UI. Business rules are not affected by a user interface (UI) requirement.

4. Independent of the database. Business rules are independent of the database implementation. It is the database that adapts to pre-existing rules.

5. Independent of any external components. The same rule applies as we commented on the database, but relating to external components, such as interactions between systems, libraries, etc.

Implementing software architecture helps us better understand what our software is about, focusing on the domain of our application. After all, this is the real value an IT company can deliver to customers. The importance of software architecture is that it enables the creation of predictive and logically organized systems.

Rich models based on our domain make all team members share the same vocabulary and consistency in naming concepts, which directly facilitates collective understanding. It also helps to have code that is easier to maintain, test, and therefore helps us meet SOLID principles:

Single Responsibility Principle

Open / Closed Principle

Liskov Substitution Principle

Interface Segregation Principle

Dependency Inversion Principle

Designing a software architecture is vital for the interests of all stakeholders involved to be considered. About the agents, understand who they are: the users of the software, the software itself, and the business objectives. Each establishes requirements and restrictions that must be taken into account in the software architecture. Obviously, at some point, the requirements may conflict.

For users, it is important for software to respond to interaction fluidly, while for business purposes, it is important that software costs little. Users may first want to implement features that are useful for day-to-day work, while software may have priority in implementing features that allow it to define its structure.

The ultimate goal of architecture is to identify requirements that affect software structure and reduce the risks associated with software development. The architecture must support future (often occurring) customer-required software, hardware, and functionality changes.

Let's summarize, then, that software architecture should have the following features:

- Show the structure of the software, but without showing the details;

- Design and design all use cases;

- Satisfy the interests of the agents as much as possible;

- Take care of functional and quality requirements;

- Determine the type of software to be developed;

- Determine the architectural styles that will be used;

- Address key cross-cutting issues.

It is the architect's responsibility to analyze the impact of his design decisions and to make a compromise between the different quality requirements as well as the commitments necessary to satisfy users, software, and business objectives.

References

https://www.researchgate.net/publication/222544881_Architecting_f
or_usability_A_survey

https://www.researchgate.net/publication/35972567_Thinking_mod
el_and_tools_for_understanding_user_experience_related_to_
information_appliance_product_concepts

http://www.interactionarchitect.com/future/vision20000202shd.htm

https://www.researchgate.net/figure/User-experience-components-
by-Arhippainen-Taehti-2003_fig4_27516496

https://www.nngroup.com/articles/usability-101-introduction-to-
usability/

https://www.researchgate.net/figure/User-Experience-Honeycomb-
Morville-2004_fig2_326735386

https://twitter.com/unclebobmartin

http://blog.cleancoder.com/

https://en.wikipedia.org/wiki/Test_double

https://meaganwaller.com/open-closed-principle-revisited/

https://stackoverflow.com/questions/36378874/   why-immutable-
objects-allow-to-comply-the-liskov-substitution-principle

https://stackoverflow.com/q/13919141

http://csci141.artifice.cc/lecture/classes.html

https://stackoverflow.com/a/44913918

http://phpdeveloper.org/tag/open

https://stackoverflow.com/questions/44913665/ how-can-i-validate-a-copy-constructors-parameter/44913805

https://docs.roguewave.com/en/jviews/8.10/jviews-maps810/samples/ jsf-maps-tiled/srchtml/demo/ViewConfigurationBean.java.html

https://github.com/p0w34007/ebooks/blob/master/Eric%20Evans%202003%20-%20Domain-Driven%20Design%20-%20Tackling%20Complexity%20in%20the%20Heart%20of%20Software.pdf

https://stackoverflow.com/questions/14831606/what-is-gang-of-four-design-pattern

https://www.springer.com/gp/book/9780792386667

https://clearmeasure.com/

https://jeffreypalermo.com/